BASIC COMPUTER KNOWLEDGE

Discipleship Press

Web: www.discipleshippress.wordpress.com
Email: maluthabiel@gmail.com
Phone: +254 797 624 994

~~***~~

P.O. Box 28448-00100, Nairobi, Kenya

ISBN-13: 9781520259314

CONTENTS

Introduction to Basic Computer Knowledge

Computer is an electronic device, which can receive data, and then process it to give out the required information. Because a computer needs electricity to work, it is an electric device. There are many types of computers, determined by their size and function. Nowadays, there are many types of personal computers.

A computer is made up of two components: hardware and software. The hardware is what we can see and touch. The software is made up of soft programs that help us perform certain actions with a computer. There are two main types of computer software: operating system software and application software. There is general as well as specific application software.

The hardware part of a computer is made up of several elements, such as monitor, Central Processing Unit (CPU) motherboard, keyboard, hard disk, mouse, memory chips, and other components. Other objects, such as printers, game devices, and scanners are also connected to a computer, in order for us to do some work. There are both input and output devices.

In this book, we will discuss some Windows versions. These are operating system software by Microsoft. The book also discusses some application software, such as word processors, and basic graphics software.

BOOK 1: WINDOWS 7 FOR BEGINNERS

INTRODUCTION TO WINDOWS 7

Windows 7 is one of the operating system software, created by Microsoft. Operating System Software manages hardware and all application software tools, installed on a computer. In this first part of the book, we will go directly into the components that make Windows 7 what it is. Windows 7 was created after Windows Vista. Before Visa, there were many other versions, such as XP, 2000, 98 and others. Actually, Windows started with Windows 01, back in 1980s!

How to Work with Windows (Any Edition)

Introduction

This simple tutorial is meant for absolute beginners in computers and how to use one. If everything here is too basic for you, you can skip it for other lessons or suggest a topic for me to cover in the other tutorials.

Thank you!

How to Turn On/Off Windows

To turn on your computer, use the power button. This button can be located on the front part of your computer case, but this depends on your machine's design.

When you locate it, just press it once, and then wait for Windows to turn on. However, when you want to turn off the computer normally, do not press the power button. Rather, click on the **Start button**, select **Power**, and then select, **Shut down**.

Related: Technology Ultimate Guide

Your machine may ask you to close running programs or save some work before it will shut down. Do what it says and the system shut down process starts.

How to Login/Log Out of Windows

When you have successfully turned on your PC (Personal Computer), it is time to login. If you have been using this computer before, then you already know how to login.

To login, simply provide your password or PIN and you will be there in no time. If you are using this machine for the first time, you will need to create a user account with a username and a password.

*You will have to be an admin to create and manage user accounts!

What Is Clicking?

Now, before you even do most of the things on a computer, and before we learn more below, it is very important to understand how to use a mouse.

A computer mouse is an input device. In laptops, it is a built-in feature, meaning you do not have to install anything before you use this input device or feature.

Nevertheless, if you have an external mouse whether wireless or wired, you will have to learn its features.

A mouse has three buttons: the left (primary button), right (secondary button), and finally, the scroll button.

To press the left mouse button once and release it, is called, single-clicking, left-clicking, or just clicking. When I tell you to click, I mean to press the left mouse button once and then release it.

To press and then release the left mouse button twice and quickly, it is double-clicking. When you do this three times, it is triple-clicking.

For example, if you want to select the whole paragraph of text, you triple-click a word in that paragraph. To select only that word, you double-click on it. To place a blinking cursor (|) on that word or any location, you single-click that place/space or word.

The Desktop Features

Here, we will look at the computer desktop features in the Widows operating system. Bear in mind that I was using Windows 10 for this tutorial. This means the images you see below (if any) will look different if you are using Windows 7 or 8, or any other earlier versions of Windows. However, the message is the same: desktop features.

The desktop in this context is that area with icons, a desktop background, and other items. We will look at those items in details below. An icon is simply a small picture that represents either a program file or a document file. There are many different kinds of files. A folder is literally a container or a directory where you keep files and other folders.

Next, we will learn how to open a program.

How Do You Open a Program?

First, there are several ways to launch or open a program installed on your computer. To install a program before you use it, see my Advanced Computer Training guides. Second, a computer program is simply a set of instructions that the machine will take in a certain order as the user wishes. In this case, there are many different programs already installed on your computer. However, the common programs are word processors, for example, Microsoft Word, WordPad, Notepad, etc. I wrote this tutorial using a Microsoft Word program.

Third, there are three basic ways to open/launch a program. The first one is to open it from the **Start Menu**. The second one is from the **Taskbar**. The third one is to open it either from the desktop, using a shortcut icon, or opening it in a folder. The first two options use a single-click process to open a program.

To open a program on the Start Menu:

1. Click on the **Start Button**
2. Look for the **Program** to open
3. **Left-click** once on its icon and it will begin to open.

To open a program on the Taskbar:

1. Locate the program icon on the **Taskbar**.
2. **Left-click** on its icon once and it will open.

To open a program on the desktop/in a folder:

1. Locate the program short cut icon on the desktop
2. Double-click on its icon to open it.
3. Double-click on the folder to see the program icon in it.
4. Double-click on the program's short cut icon in the folder to open it.

To open a program from the Search Menu:

1. Click on the **Search Menu** next to the **Start Button**.
2. Type the program name.
3. Select the program in the search results.
4. Then the program will begin to open.
5. Wait for the program as it may take a moment to load/launch.

How Do You Create a File?

Even before we learn how to create, a file as discussed above, it is good to learn how to create one, isn't it? Now, let us learn how to create a file. A file in this case is an item that contains some data. For example, this tutorial is a file, which contains text for showing you how to do these tasks on a computer.

You can create a file in several ways. One way to create a file is by opening a program as we have learned above. After a program is open, we can use its menu to open a previous file create with the same program.

Now, a file has to be associated with the right program on your computer in order for you to open it. For example, you can open the Word version of this program with Microsoft Word, or with any other word processor, which is compatible with this file type. You cannot create a program file using this tutorial.

To create a word file document from the Start Menu:

1. Click on the Start Button.
2. Locate the Word Program.
3. Single-click on its icon.
4. Choose a blank template.
5. Type your words.
6. Click on the Save button on the Quick Access Toolbar
7. Give your file a name to remember it later.
8. Select a drive to save it on and click on the Save button to close the save menu.

To create a word file document from the Desktop:

1. Right-click somewhere empty on the desktop.
2. Choose New.
3. Select Microsoft Word Document in the menu.
4. Type your desired name to replace the New Microsoft Word Document name.
5. Click anywhere outside the new file name to save it.

To open a file from the Search Menu:

1. Left-click on the **Search Button** next to the Start Button.
2. Type the file name.
3. Left-click on the file to pen it.
4. Click Open file location to know where the file sits on your computer.

To create a folder on the Desktop:

1. Right-click on the desktop (not on a shortcut icon, file or folder).
2. In the secondary menu that appears, select **New**.
3. Point to **Folder** and left-click it.
4. Type a new name of your choice for the folder to replace the **New Folder** placeholder text.
5. Single-click anywhere outside the folder name to save it.

To create a folder in another folder:

1. Double-click the mother folder to open it.
2. Right-click somewhere empty within the open folder.
3. In the secondary menu that appears, select **New**.
4. Point to **Folder** and left-click it.
5. Type a new name of your choice for the folder to replace the **New Folder** placeholder text.
6. Single-click anywhere outside the folder name to save it.

You can also create folders in which you can keep other folders and all kinds of files in them. In my series, you will learn about file types and file name extensions.

How Do You Save a File?

We have already seen how to save a file above after creating it. A file can be either a folder file, a word document file, or a program file. We cannot create a program file and save it in this tutorial, but we might have downloaded it from the Internet or email. We might also want to save a file on a different folder or drive within the same machine.

To save a file from an email message:

1. Click the download button next to the file.
2. On the save dialogue box choose a folder or directory.
3. Click **Save**.

To save a file to a different drive:

1. Open the file (see how above)
2. On the file menu, select Save As.
3. Select the drive (e.g. **D:**...)
4. Click **Save**.

To copy a file to a different folder:

1. Locate the file you want to copy.
2. If the file is in a folder, open that folder (learn how above)
3. If on the desktop, locate it there.
4. Single-click the file to select it.
5. Move to the folder where you want to save the file.
6. Press **CTRL+V** to paste the file and save it there.

How Do You Retrieve a File?

To retrieve a file means to locate or find it where it was previously saved. We have already learned how to open a file above, and this means we have learned where it is saved. In this section, we will learn some more ways to find and open a saved file or folder.

To retrieve a saved file on your computer:

1. Double-click on the Computer (This PC) shortcut icon on the desktop.
2. Single-click Documents.
3. Scroll down in that folder to see the document file (if it was saved here), or
4. Single-click Pictures and look for it there if it was a picture.

To retrieve a saved file on a Flash Disk:

1. Double-click on the Computer (This PC) shortcut icon on the desktop.
2. Single-click on the drive letter for your Pen Drive/Flash Disk (e.g. **F:**).
3. Scroll down to see the file if you cannot see it.

How Do You Transfer a File?

There are several ways to transfer a file to another location either on the same computer or to an external drive or email. First, you have to access the file or files that you want to send or transfer before you begin the transfer process as shown below.

To transfer a file to another drive or folder:

1. Left-click the file or files to select it or them.
2. Right-click on the selected file or files.
3. Choose "**Send to**" in the list that will appear.
4. Select the folder or drive you want to send or transfer the file or files to.

To copy and paste a file or files from and to a drive or folder:

1. Select the file or files.
2. Right-click on the selected file or files.
3. Select "**Copy**" in the menu that will appear.
4. Navigate to the other new folder or drive.
5. Right-click anywhere in the new folder or drive.
6. Left-click "**Paste**" to place the file or files in the new folder or drive.

How Do You Attach a File?

To attach a file or folder means to add it into something else such as an email message. This is part of the Internet usage especially when it comes to file sharing and communication skills. You might have already known that a computer is a multipurpose device that we use for different purposes.

To attach and send a file:

1. Open your email client software for example, Mail or Chrome.
2. Sign in to your email account using username and password.
3. Create/compose a new email message.
4. Click the paperclip icon.
5. Select the file from your computer/phone and it will attach.

How Do You Update Your Computer?

Updating your computer is a security activity that is recommended. Even if you have an active antivirus program, you still need to update the operating software itself. This is great especially if you are using Windows as your operating system.

To update Windows and other programs/applications:

1. Make sure your computer has strong internet connection such as Wi-Fi.
2. Click on the **Start button**.
3. Type the word, "**Update**" without quotes.
4. Select "**Check for update,**" in the results that will show up.
5. Left-click "**Check for updates**" in the settings app.

Wait for updates to download and install automatically.

CHAPTER 1: THE DESKTOP

Figure 1: Windows 7 Desktop

What is a desktop, and where is it located on a computer? According to Microsoft Help and Support:

> *A desktop is the work area on a computer screen where you can put things that you want easy access to, just as you arrange objects on top of your actual desk. On your computer desktop, you can arrange icons such as the Recycle Bin and shortcuts to programs, folders and documents or other files"*—Microsoft Help and Support 2012.

I think this is more than a definition, because it gives us a clear example of what a desktop is. You can see how important a desktop is on a computer. It is the first screen that you see, when you log on to your computer or when you turn on your computer. We will explore the important parts of a desktop in Windows 7 and these are **Icons, Gadgets, Taskbar, Start Button**, and Wallpaper/desktop background.

ICONS

What are icons and how do they look like? According to Microsoft Help and Support: *"An icon is a small picture that represents a file, folder, program, or other object or function."*

This means there are many different icons for different things on a desktop. You can have shortcut icons or real file icons, as well as program icons. A file icon represents a program used to create that file. For example, a Word Document icon looks like the Microsoft Word program and this is how you can tell the differences between icon types.

Any program has its own icon that makes it different from other programs. Microsoft Office Access and Microsoft Word icons are not the same, because these are different programs. An icon can represent a picture or an image, because there are many programs that can open image files.

The default program you use to open image files on your computer can only determine the icon for a particular image on your desktop. The common programs to open an image file with are programs such as Windows Photo Viewer, Microsoft Office Picture Manager, Paint, or Windows Media Centre. There are many other photo editing programs or software for free or for purchase such as Adobe Photoshop.

There are also different types of images, depending on how you took the picture and the device you used to capture that picture. File icons also contain file names. An advanced computer user can decide whether a file name extension will be visible or invisible, using a feature known as, **"folder options."** Below are some examples of icons on your desktop screen.

Figure 2: Recycle Bin

This icon above represents a program called, **Recycle Bin**, and you can use **Windows Explorer** to open this directory. It is a location where deleted items are kept until you finally delete them.

The Recycle Bin is not really a program, but it is a directory or a folder on your computer and it is always located somewhere on your desktop. You can see that this glass-like icon shows that the folder is not empty because there are deleted items in it.

Figure 3: Computer Icon

This is a computer icon on your desktop. In Windows Vista or Windows 7, you choose whether you want this icon to be on your desktop or not. This is a location for all your hard disk drives such as **C: Drive** where Windows files are stored by default.

Double-clicking on this icon opens a computer folder, where you can see connected devices. This is not just a shortcut icon, but also a real program icon. You can open this location or folder, using **Windows Explorer**, a program that always comes installed with your computer.

Figure 4: Kindle for PC

Amazon Kindle is a software I use for reading e-books on my laptop computer, and this is the icon for that program (Figure 4). This icon is a shortcut icon, because it is not a real icon for this program. I know that this is a shortcut icon, because it has an arrow pointing upwards to the picture. This icon and other icons are always located on the computer desktop for ease of access to the real program. You can even have folders on the desktop, and these folders are always represented by a folder icon.

Any file or program on a computer must be stored somewhere on your computer, and when a file is on a desktop, you can point to it and the computer will tell you the location of that file.

Figure 5: Desktop Icon

The above folder is named after desktop icons, and it was located on my desktop screen. Even this real folder icon can be placed on the desktop as you can see above, or I can even make a shortcut of the same folder and place it on the desktop as well.

Now, you can see that we can have many different icons for different programs on the desktop, depending on the need of a computer user. Real files or folders can be placed on a desktop, if the user wants to do so. I can place my Microsoft Word file on the desktop, if I want to do so.

However, for me, I like placing files in folders, and I also place folders a library, not on my desktop, because I don't want to place my folders on the desktop, since it looks bad for me. We will soon discuss the wallpaper, which is part of the desktop.

If you ever used a mobile phone before, or any electronic device, you already know what the wallpaper is. It is the background picture on your computer's desktop. A desktop is the first window you see when you turn on your computer before any program opens.

WALLPAPERS

If you are a mobile phone user, you already know about wallpapers, right? The same thing applies to the computer, whether laptop or desktop. Wallpaper is a picture or an image that you can place on your desktop. You can put any picture to your desktop, if you want to do so. Many types of wallpapers come installed with Windows, and the easy way to find them in Windows 7 is following simple steps below. Right-click on your desktop and point to the **personalize** link at the bottom of the list that appears on your desktop. Now, click on **personalize** link and then you will see the wallpapers in different types. The common types of wallpapers are: **My Themes**, **Aero Themes**, and then **Basic** and **High Contrast Themes**. Under each theme type, you can choose one or all the theme pictures, and the theme will be applied to your desktop background as soon as you click on it. Under my themes, you can save new themes or get some free from the Microsoft website, and begin to use them.

You must have a good and up to date antivirus program before you download anything from the Internet. I do not encourage you to download anything, even if it is on the Microsoft website. Be careful when you download anything because you may get infected with viruses without your knowledge. Viruses are malicious programs that look like real programs, but they are designed to harm you or your computer. Some are used to steal your personal details—contact information.

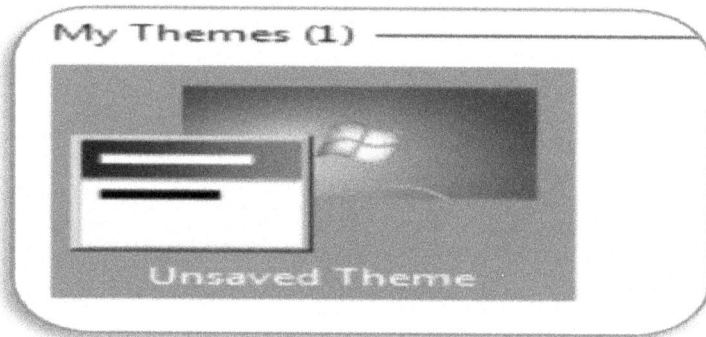

Figure 6: My Themes

This is an example of **My Themes** type of wallpapers on the computer. This is an **unsaved theme**, because I did not give it a name as you can see on the picture above. There is only one (1) theme in this location, but I can add more themes or pictures, even from my computer. Any picture I set as wallpaper becomes one of my themes, and I can get it here.

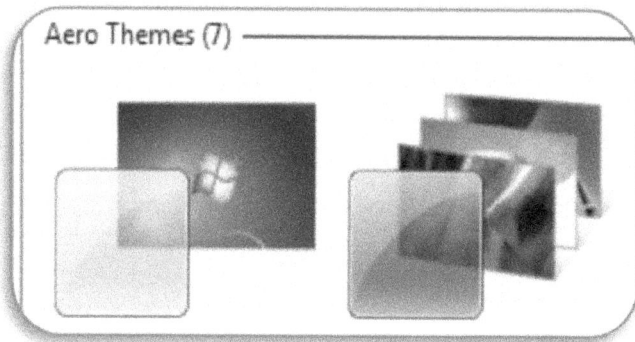

Figure 7: Aero Themes

In **Aero Themes**, there are seven (7) themes as you can see above, but I must use one wallpaper at a time. If I want to change the current theme, I only have to click on a different wallpaper, and wait for a few seconds for the wallpaper to get activated.

There is also **Basic** or **High** contrast theme type, and I can use only one theme type at a time, if I want to do so. You remember that the way to see these themes or wallpapers is to follow the steps above. This process of opening the themes is the same in Windows XP, Vista and Windows 7. In Windows XP, you have to click, **Properties**, not **Personalize** link as in Windows Vista and Windows 7. A screen saver is also part of a wallpaper or theme. You can set the screen saver in the same way you created wallpaper, just by clicking the screen saver link and follow the onscreen instructions.

GADGETS

Gadgets are not the same as wallpapers or themes. They are links, representing some computer programs on your computer. Windows comes loaded with some desktop gadgets, but you have to activate them, if you want.

To get gadgets, just click on the **Start Button** and on the list that jumps up on the left, click on the desktop gadgets and wait as they open up (Windows Sidebar in Vista). Now, you can choose which gadget you want, and to activate one, just double-click on it and it will show up on the right side of your desktop screen. You can still drag or move the gadget to a place you want it to be on your desktop.

You can set a gadget or customize it, to make it look the way you want, but this depends on the gadget type you have on your computer. Besides using the Windows desktop gadgets, you can also use your own gadgets, if you can download some from a website (trusted ones).

Figure 8: Clock Gadget

This is a clock gadget on my desktop (Figure 7). The user to the desktop as mentioned earlier must add the gadget. The main use of a gadget is for you to get access to the tools you need such as a clock or calendar.

You can add gadgets to the desktop screen for different programs that have gadget features. Not all programs have gadget features. In short, gadgets are special computer programs, designed to be displayed on a desktop screen for quick access.

Figure 9: Calendar Gadget

This was my calendar gadget. I use it as a normal calendar on the wall or on my table as you can see above. I can even expand this calendar if I want to see the days. To do that, I have to click on a certain button near the gadget in order for me to change the settings or options.

There are always three buttons next to a gadget, normally on the top-right corner. These buttons help you drag, expand or close a gadget. You can make a gadget look small or big by using the **Expand** button, normally in the middle. Instead of using the **Drag** and **Drop** buttons, you can also click directly on a gadget and drag and then drop it somewhere on the desktop.

Figure 10: MSDN

This is my Microsoft Developer Network gadget on my desktop (Figure 9). This program is useful for me, because I can ask a question on the MSDN website by clicking on the right button as shown above.

I can click and open the forum questions very easily, using this feature. I can even see my thread updates, or set a support priority, meaning I can see my interest areas and topics on the same MSDN website. When I click there, the computer will open the interest area or topic on the Microsoft website. I can even search the website for any question, by typing the question in the search box on the gadget.

I can then click the search icon, or I can just press the enter key on my computer keyboard, to start searching the MSDN website. I can even click the **Home** button or the **Messaging** button on the gadget, if I want to do so, and the computer will do just what I want it to do for me. You can now see that there are many gadgets for different programs and you can use them for different things. Gadgets are also called, **Desktop Gadgets**, because you only use them on a desktop. Gadgets are real programs, designed in a way that they can be used on a desktop, just as you can use a shortcut icon to open a real file or program, stored on your computer.

START BUTTON

The Start Button is a very important part of a computer because as the name suggests, it is where you *start* almost everything on your computer. We use the Start Button to start many programs that do not have their shortcut icons on a desktop as discussed earlier. The Start Button is part of a desktop, located on the far bottom-left corner of a computer screen. It is part of the Taskbar and the Taskbar is part of the desktop. We will discuss more about this feature in Windows 7, just below. The Start Button deserves a section by itself, because it has many features on it that need to be discussed properly.

We will soon discuss the Taskbar. As the name suggests, a Taskbar is a place where you can see all the tasks you are currently carrying out, such as open windows and other items you are working with. Any opened program or file will show up on the Taskbar of your computer. You can see the Taskbar picture as shown below in figure 10.

TASKBAR

A Taskbar is part of a desktop of your computer screen. Remember, the term **Desktop** here does not refer to the type of a computer, but to any monitor or screen of any computer, being a laptop or desktop, or even a Tablet PC. The Taskbar is located on a bottom part of any desktop screen, but you can decide where you want to locate yours. The Taskbar as the name suggests, contains open programs and files, and when you minimize any window, it will sit right on your computer Taskbar, until you click on it again to open it or maximize it. The Taskbar covers the bottom of the desktop, from left to right.

Figure 11: Taskbar

As you can see above, a Taskbar is located at the bottom of the Windows desktop screen from left to right. There are **Left**, **Centre** and **Right** sides of a Taskbar, with different icons on them. The icons on the left side of a Taskbar are representing pinned programs, or opened programs. This Windows feature of pinning programs to the Taskbar is found in Windows Vista, Windows 7 and Windows XP.

The design for the Taskbar in Windows XP is different from the one for Windows 7. By default, programs like your web browser such as **Internet Explorer**, **Windows Explorer** and other programs, are pinned on the Taskbar. You can remove pinned programs by right-clicking on them, and then choose **unpin** this program from Taskbar options and the program is unpinned, just as easy as that. In the middle of the Taskbar is where you can add other things such as links, toolbars and other items.

This centre area can also get full with pinned programs, if you pin many of them, and they can start from left to the middle of the

20

Taskbar. But there is a limit of pinned programs, where only an arrow can point up, if the limit area is reached. And if you want to see all pinned programs you have to click on that arrow pointing upwards mostly on the left side of the Taskbar. The right side of the Taskbar is called, **Notification Area**. Under notification area, there is a "time/clock button" and desktop icons, where you can set the time or clock button and date of your machine.

You can customize the **Notification Area** by choosing the show icons and notifications, or show only notifications. This area of Windows Taskbar is very important, because it is where you can see alerts from Action Centre, a feature in Windows that helps you take care of your computer—Security Centre.

By default, the network meter, battery meter, and audio icons are shown in the notification area. Nevertheless, you can remove or add more icons by clicking the arrow that points upwards in the notification area. Then click, **customize...** blue link where the customizing options window will show up. Set your notification area and click the **OK** button. You will see the customizing window below—figure 11. If you choose, **always show all icons and notifications on the Taskbar**, your Taskbar will be full of many icons, which you may not need. I do not recommend this, anyway.

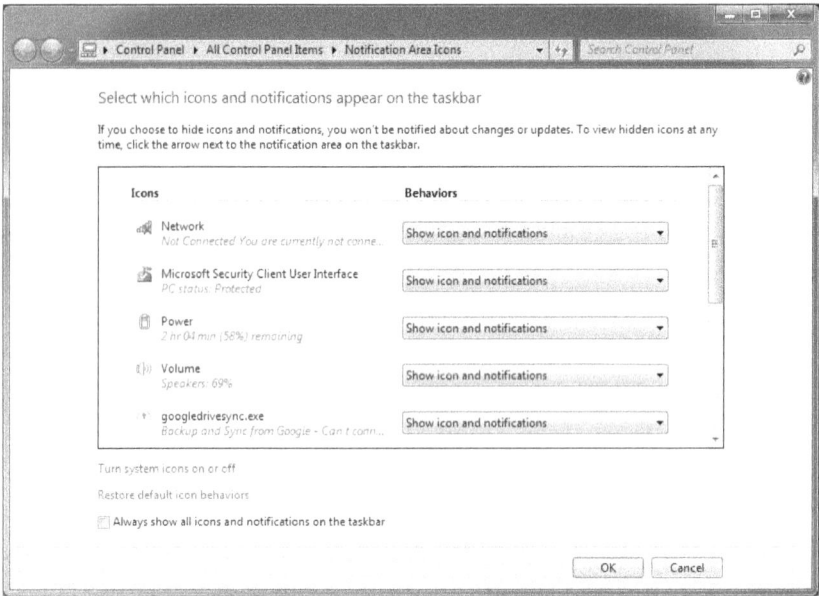

Figure 12: Notification settings

In this picture, you can see two things: **Icons** and **Behaviours**. The icons are on the left, and their behaviours are on the right. You can there choose what you want to happen to a particular icon in the notification area, as shown above.

I suggest you set the notification alert for your antivirus to be showing both the icon and the notification at the same time, so that you always know what is happening on your computer. If you right-clicked on the centre of the Taskbar, you will see links or options such as toolbars, address, links, Tablet PC Input Panel, desktop, and new toolbar.

This is where you can add almost any folder to the taskbar as a toolbar for easy access. This does not mean that you will have the folders on the Taskbar; but you will have links to folders on the Taskbar. There are many options to choose from, when you choose to right-click on the centre of the Taskbar, especially if there are many open programs or windows on your computer at that time.

These options include, cascade windows, show windows stacked, show windows side by side, and show desktop.

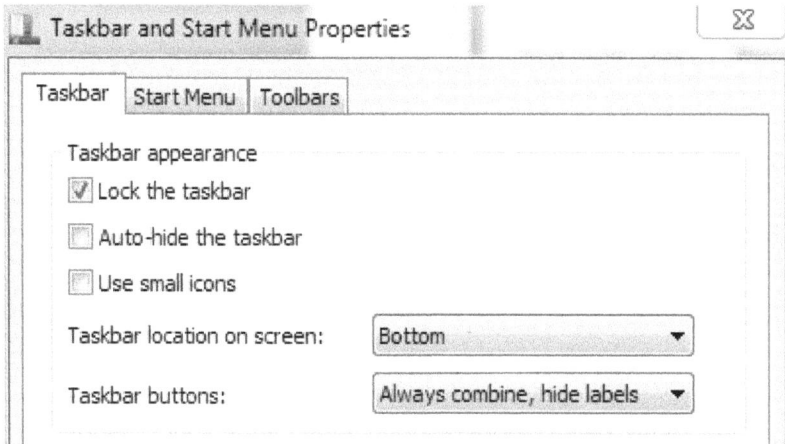

Figure 13: Taskbar Tab

You can even choose to log the Taskbar, or start the Task Manager, a feature in Windows that makes you able to view all the running processes and programs on your machine at the same time. You can even choose the Taskbar Properties, and this is one place where you can do many things at once for your taskbar including the customization of your taskbar. If you click **Properties**, the window to the taskbar and the Start Menu properties will open as shown above.

There are three tabs on the window above, and these are, **Taskbar**, **Start Menu**, and **Toolbars**. You can click on any of the three to see many options and settings under it. Under the Taskbar properties, you can log the taskbar, auto-hide the Taskbar or use small icons on the Taskbar. If you cannot see all these in the picture above, please consider doing it on your computer practically. You can also choose where you want your Taskbar to appear on the desktop. By default, the Taskbar appears on the bottom of the desktop screen.

But you can place it on the right, left or on top of the desktop screen, just by choosing the place and click the **Apply** button to see what happens before you click the **Ok** button. You can even change the Taskbar buttons' appearance from here by choosing **always combine, hide labels** or **combine when Taskbar is full**, or even you can choose **never combine icon** option. It is good to use the first option above, so that when icons from the same program are opened, they will be placed in one place, where you can easily find them on your Taskbar.

Again, you can customize the **Notification Area** and icons that appear on it right here under that taskbar tab. There is always a link with the question "How do I customize the taskbar?" And you can use this link to learn more about this feature, and the help files will open from your computer. On the Start Menu tab you can customize how the links, icons and menus look and behave in the Start Menu.

You can even choose what the power button does, when clicked. You will need to see figure 13 for more information about how to setup the Start Menu and privacy of your computer. The Start Menu tab on the Taskbar and Start Menu window is always found under the properties of the Taskbar. As mentioned elsewhere in this book, you can open the Taskbar properties window by right-clicking the Taskbar and then choose properties from the drop-down menu.

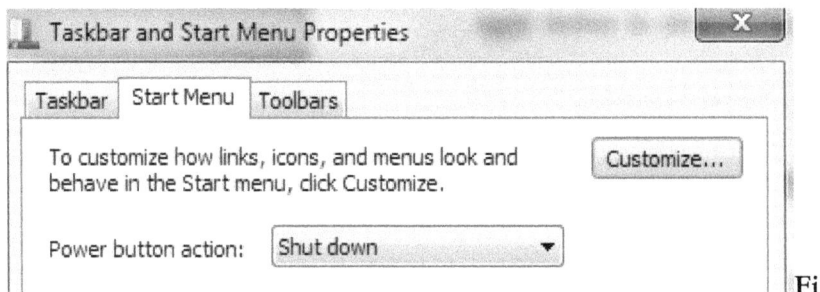

gure 14: Start Menu Tab

The power button action is set to **Shut down** by default, but you can change the action from here to anything you like, such as switch user, hibernate, log off, lock, restart and many other actions, and the button will do what you want it to do, when clicked after you saved the changes.

You can choose the privacy settings such as **store and display recently opened programs in the Start Menu.** You can choose to display **recently opened items in the Start Menu and Taskbar.** But sometimes any user can open your important documents! So be careful with this option.

The last tab in the list of properties is the toolbar tab. This is where you can choose to add other items to the Taskbar, such as an address. This is where you can type and such for many things on your computer, if you want to search for a file or program instead of using the Start Menu and the search box under it.

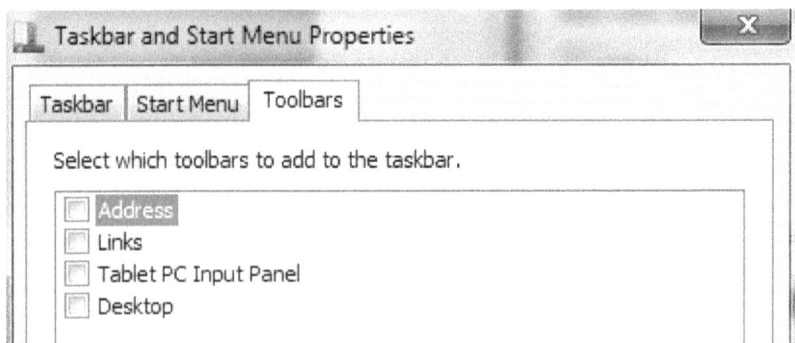

Figure 15: Toolbar Tab

You can add many things to the Taskbar here, such as address, links, tablet PC Input Panel, and desktop. The Tablet PC Input is a panel where you can use a program such as Windows Journal, which helps you use the on-screen keyboard and a handwriting on certain computers with touch screens. The Tablet PC program can help you write on your computer, using a handwriting style, and then convert that into a text that will look like a typed work, and this is fun isn't it? The desktop toolbar will just add anything on the desktop or any folder you chose to the Taskbar. This is in a form of a link, and when clicked, you can browse into any part of your computer, including the connected drives, just from the Taskbar.

This is the **Toolbars** tab above, and the picture shows that the desktop link is selected (checked). When the changes are saved after selecting the desktop as shown above, you can see the desktop toolbar added to the right side of the Taskbar, just before the notification area.

This has not only linked to the desktop, but to the whole computer. All the drives can be accessed from the Taskbar after adding the desktop toolbar to the Taskbar as shown above. It depends on your need, if you can activate one or all the features on the Toolbars tab on figure 14 above. I like the desktop tool/link even though I do not use it a lot, because it gives you the easiest way to find folders on your computer.

If you want to practice several ways of setting this feature, follow some steps below. You can right-click the Taskbar, choose the Toolbars on the menu, always on top, choose an address, or links, or desktop, Tablet PC Input Panel or just the New Toolbar. The New toolbar here allows you to choose any folder or drive on your computer to add to the toolbar. When you clicked on the 'New toolbar' link, you can browse to any directory or place on your computer, to choose a folder to add to the Taskbar. There are many other options to choose from, when you right-click the Taskbar.

You can cascade windows, show windows stacked, show windows side-by-side, show the desktop, start Task Manager or lock the Taskbar. Most of the options above appear only when many windows are open. You can still open or launch the Task Manager, even if no windows are open. However, you cannot show windows side by side unless some windows are open on the Taskbar. As mentioned earlier, you can also get to the Taskbar and Start Menu setup window from the Taskbar. How do you do this? Just right-click the **Taskbar**, and choose **Properties** in the drop-down menu.

TEST YOURSELF

1. What is a **Desktop?**
2. What is **Wallpaper?**
3. What are **Icons?**
4. Set or change your **Desktop Background**.
5. Open your **Desktop Gadgets**.
6. What is **Shortcut Icon?**
7. What is **Start Button**, and where is it located?
8. What is **Taskbar**, and where is it located?
9. Change your **Taskbar** location.

CHAPTER 2: THE START BUTTON

As mentioned in the first chapter, the Start Button is very important in computing, because almost everything starts from here, just as the name suggests. There are many features on the Start Button, and we are going to discuss them shortly.

The features include the **Search box, Start Menu, Commands, Links** and **All Programs**. All of these are found under the **Start Button**. We will not show all these links and commands, using the pictures or illustrations here, but I expect you to read and practice what you are learning by putting it into practice right now.

Click on the **Start Button** and you will begin to see many links. We are going to explore those links and features right now.

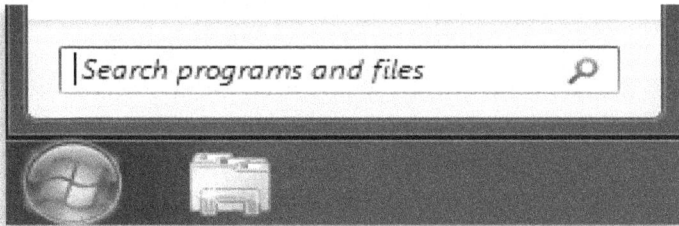

The Start menu search box

Figure 16: Start Menu Search Box

A **Search box** is a box above the **Start Button**, which can help you search every location on your computer. This can help you search for files and programs, that you cannot remember where to find them after a long time of not checking or using them. I sometimes forget where I saved my documents, and I have to use the **Search box**, to get that particular document. You can sometimes forget where your important document is, because you cannot find it after searching for it almost everywhere on your computer. If this is your problem right now, just follow these simple steps and you will soon get your files in less than a minute's time.

This icon represents the Start Button. This Start Button is always located on the far left-bottom of the computer screen, even though you may decide to place it somewhere else on the desktop, as discussed above—Taskbar (Figure 10). If you want to start finding and using your programs, just press on the icon you see above, using the left mouse button and you will see the list of your installed programs.

For now, we want to look at the **Search box**. Click on the **Start Button** and you will see the box just above the **Start Button**, but under **All Programs** link, and this box have a text on it that reads *"Search programs and files,"* (See figure 15 above). Have you seen that? If yes, then just begin typing the name of your lost files, and soon you will see the results above the search box.

Listen now, if you see the file you are looking for, do not left-click on it, because this will only open the file, but you will not be sure where the file is stored on your computer. Instead, click the file link, using the right mouse button (right-clicking) and choose the **Open file location** option, and that will take you to the folder, a drive where the actual file is located—real file. Did you get your file? That is great! This is the reason why this guide was written because I realized that many people are still having problems on how to use computers, and you may be one of the victims, and if this is the case, then this book is for you.

You may then want to help others, sharing your experience with them. Now, we move on to other topics under the **Start Button**, as I said earlier when the topic started. Here, we are going to talk about the **Start Menu** a menu under the **Start Button** itself. Do you want to know about this menu? Read on to the other pages and get educated. As mentioned earlier, there are many links below **Start Button**.

START MENU

The **Start Menu** is also known as **Quick List**, because when you click on the **Start Button**, a list opens above, and this list is the **Start Menu**. It contains links commands and even the most important link, **All Programs**. We will look at these links below in more details. Depending on your personal settings, your **Start Menu** may contain different items.

There can be many or a few items on your **Start Menu** as the result of what you set, using the **Taskbar and Start Menu** setup window as discussed earlier in this book (Figure 12). If I want my computer to show the recently opened files, then there will be many items on my **Start Menu**, depending on how many programs were recently opened.

Figure 18: Start Menu

The **Start Menu** can be divided into two sections: right and left. All these links on the **Start Menu** are kinds of commands, because when clicked, they run a command in the computer memory, just like any other computer program. You can even run the **Command Prompt** from here, if you type the program file, and it will open or run. We are not going to run a **Command Prompt**.

COMMANDS

As you can see above, commands are those links on the **Start Menu**. These are links that you can click to do certain work on the computer (If you did not log off). The left side section of the Start Menu contains all currently opened programs. These are programs that have been opened recently, and depending on your **Start**

Menu settings, these links can allow you to open recently opened files on your computer, without you going to the file location.

The risk of this is that anyone using your computer may open your files without going to your account folders! This also depends on your Start Menu settings as discussed above. You can learn many things about computing, but be careful not to corrupt your computer. You have to go with me systematically. Do not try to run commands here, if you do not know what you are trying to do with them, because any advanced command you run can confuse your computer in just a few seconds, and the result is that your machine may not work.

Links

Links are always located on the right side of the Start Menu. There are many links by default, added to the **Start Menu**, such as a link to your current User Account, Documents, Pictures, Music, Computer, Control Panel, Devices and Printers, Default Programs and then Help and Support links. Clicking on each link makes your computer do what you want it to do for you.

There are nine links on the **Start Menu** of any computer, running on Windows Vista or Windows 7, when you clicked on the **Start Menu**. Four of these links open real folders, when clicked, but five links open Control Panel folders. The computer link opens a computer folder in the Control Panel. The Devices and Printers or Default Programs, plus Control Panel links open folders that are part of the Control Panel folders on the computer. You have to be very careful with such links, because they can allow you to open critical parts of your computer, such as the Control Panel, where you can mess up with your machine, if you are just a beginner in computers.

Before we discuss, **All Programs** on the Start Menu, I want to tell you something about one important button on the Start Menu.

This button is where the power button actions are located and this is good for us to discuss right now. This button by default contains the words **Shut down**, but you can change these words to something else as discussed earlier in the book (Figure 12). Next to this button, is a little arrow, pointing to the right hand side, and clicking on this little arrow opens more actions for the power button.

The actions are other commands you can run such as Switch user, Log off, Lock, Restart, Sleep or Hibernate. Sometimes, these actions may disappear because of something that happened to your computer, and for this reason, I have developed a little software called, Windows Program Launcher, that can help you in this area.

This program was designed for Windows 7, but it works perfectly in all versions of Windows 7 such as Starter, Home Basic, Home Premium, Professional, and even Windows 7 Ultimate, XP and Vista, including Windows 8 and 10. Sometimes, you may need your computer to be hibernated, so that you resume Windows when power comes back. However, you just realize that your computer is missing that feature for that particular moment. Our software mentioned above can help you in fixing this problem.

ALL PROGRAMS

This is the link above the **Search box** on the **Start Button**. The link is available in all versions of Microsoft Windows, including Windows XP. In Windows 7, you can point to the link or just click it and **All Programs** will open up on top of this link. Some programs will have folders or just icons, and you can click any program once, using the left mouse button in order to open it. This is the difference between opening a program on a desktop or in another folder, and opening it on the **Start Menu**. On the **Start Menu**, you only need to left-click on the program icon once, and the program or folder will start to open.

On the desktop or other locations, you have to double-click or left-click on a folder twice and quickly in order to open a file or folder. Depending on how many programs you have installed on your computer, you can see many programs, when you click the **All Programs** link from the **Start Menu**. In Windows XP, programs will show up on the right side of the **Start Menu**. However, on Windows Vista and Windows 7, you can see them on the left-hand side of the **Start Menu**.

If a program has a folder or folders, you will see the folders and the recently opened programs will show up on top of other programs. You can see Window 7 Control Panel (Part IV) for more information about programs and how to work with programs including installing and uninstalling programs from your computer.

TEST YOURSELF

1. What is a **Search Box** and where is it located?
2. What is a **Start Menu**?
3. What are **Commands**?
4. What are **Links**?

CHAPTER 3: FILES

You may recall that there are many different types of files. We even defined what a file is before, and now we are going to look at files in more details. We are going to look at types of files, real and shortcut files, then file endings, also known as file name extensions.

You have learned that a file is made by using a certain program, and you might have already created some files on your computer before you got this book. Files have types and their types can be determined by the program used to create them—icon and file name extension. Right-click on the **Desktop**, choose **New**, choose what file to create and then **rename** it.

Some programs are meant to open only one type of files, but some programs are meant to open many file types or files with different file name extensions. The Microsoft Word program can only open word documents, but WordPad program can open both WordPad documents, as well as Microsoft Word documents.

TYPES OF FILES

There are many types of files as mentioned above. But the most common file types are, **Program Files** and **Document Files**. A Microsoft Word document file is a document file type, created using Microsoft Word program. A program is a set of instructions, commands, or tasks that a computer can perform, when a user clicks a button on the program. Please, see the list of computing terminologies at the end of this book for more help on definitions. There are many picture or image file types, as well as program file types that we cannot discuss in this topic, simply because file types are so many. Nevertheless, you have to know that program files are files that can be executed on a machine, making a computer do certain tasks as directed by a programmer.

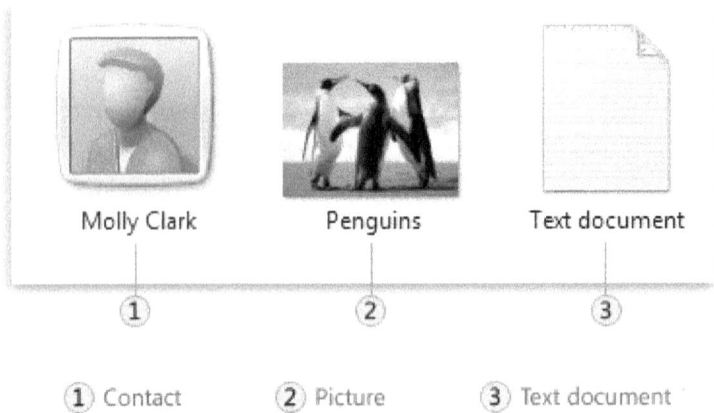

Molly Clark   Penguins   Text document

①   ②   ③

① Contact   ② Picture   ③ Text document

Icons for a few types of files

Figure 19: File Types

A programmer is either a computer's advanced user, who is trained to program a computer, or a person can learn programming alone without going to the class. I am one of such people who can make computer programs, depending on a customer's needs. I'm one of the self-learning computer programmers. I can make small programs based on my needs.

We can conclude that a file can be a picture, a document, or even a program file. But how do we know that the file is a document or program? We will learn more about file name extensions later. This will help us answer this question. You might have known this before, and if that is the case, continue reading, and you may find the right place for you in the book.

REAL FILES

Real files are actual files that are not shortcuts. We have learned earlier that shortcut files are mostly found on a desktop, but we can place shortcuts in any directory or folder on a computer, depending on the need. Any webpage file is actually a link to an actual page on the Internet. The real file can be stored on a desktop or in a folder, depending on the need of a computer user. You can create a shortcut icon from a real file. You cannot open a real file from a shortcut, if the real file is missing on your computer or drive.

SHORTCUT FILES

Shortcut files are not real files, but you can open real files using shortcut files, that represent them on your computer. If your real files are located on an external drive, you have to connect that drive to the computer, before you try to open the real file, using a shortcut link.

It doesn't matter where the real file is located on your computer, because you can still open it, using its shortcut icon. When you are saving a file from an external drive, make sure you do not create a shortcut, but to copy and paste the file to your computer, so that when that drive is removed from your computer, you can still be able to open the file. This is because you already have the real file stored there.

FILE ENDINGS

File endings are also known as file name extensions, and these are very important for a computer user like you to know. This section is a bit advanced, and if you do not understand, please try to read the section several times, until you get the point or ask someone with more computing knowledge than you do to help you.

Most common file name extensions

The following table describes file name extensions that might indicate that a file is dangerous.

Extension	Type of file
.exe	Program
.com	MS-DOS program
.pif	Shortcut to MS-DOS program
.bat	Batch file
.scr	Screen saver file

Figure 20: File name Extensions

Sometimes, it is not important to know file name extensions, but this is important, because we want to determine a file type. There are many file name extensions, depending on the program used to create the files. Image files have their own name extensions, and document or program files have their own different name extensions.

The basic truth is that any file ending with (**.exe**) is a program file. The funny thing is that Windows does not show file name extensions by default, unless you enable this feature, yourself. This takes us to advanced feature of Windows 7, something I never intended for this beginners' textbook. Please see Windows 7 Control Panel (Part IV) for this.

To enable file name extensions, left-click **Start Button**, and then type, "**Folder options**," in the Search box. Soon, you will see the link that matches your search. Click on the link, and a window will open, where you can now enable the feature that will allow your computer to show the file name extensions.

On that window that opened after clicking the folder options in the search box, click on the **View** tab, always in the middle, then click or uncheck the box where it reads "Hide file extensions for known file types," and then click the **OK** button. This will show file name extensions on your computer, and you will always see the three last letters on any file, whether on the desktop or in any folder on your computer. A file with more than one file name extension or type, also known as a file ending, must be suspected to be a virus file or the so called malicious program by computer wizards. For more information about viruses and malicious programs, see definitions at the end of this book. The file name extensions help you to identify the kind of file you are looking at or the file you are working with.

But, as mentioned earlier, there are so many file types and file name extensions, and many more are coming up. Computer programmers are making many different programs. Some computer programs are malicious, and some are good for use. The Microsoft Office programs are good for us to use, but sometimes someone with an advanced knowledge of computer can still insert a malicious code into a normal program such as Microsoft Word file.

Please, be careful with programs you do not understand. Use only the programs you know well, and do not download and install new programs from the Internet, unless you are sure of what they are.

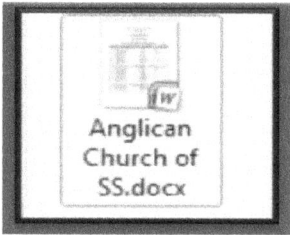

Figure 21: MS Word

This Microsoft Word file type ends with, **(.docx)** file name extension, and this tells us that the file was created with Microsoft Office Word 2007, because Office Word 2003 ends with, (.doc) filename extension. You see the difference? Even Microsoft Word program has different file name extensions such as [.doc], [.docx], or even [.rtf], which stands for rich text format. The PDF file name extension is file that can be opened by a program called, Adobe Reader. PDF is for Portable Document Format.

To learn more about many file name extensions in Microsoft Word program, just click on the Office Button. Then click on the save as, and there click the drop-down menu for the save as type and learn how many different file formats you can see from there (Word options). Are they not many? Did you know this before or is it a new idea, a discovery for you?

In short, there are so many file types or file name extensions, and it is also true that we cannot even exhaust the topic here.

Figure 22: Program file

This file above ends with (.exe) file name extension, and this tells us that the file is a program file, meaning it can be installed on a computer, if opened. Remember, a program is software, with certain tasks and commands given by the programmer of that program.

This file above represents my program. It simply reads, **Setup**, meaning you can use this single file to install many other files in the program on your computer. The function of this software is to help you use your computer in a very easy way. The actual program represented by the icon above is Windows Program Launcher, because the tool helps you open many Windows applications, just in one place, and you can have it free from our website, if you need it.

Now, you have learned more about program icons and file icons. But, as mentioned earlier, there are many file types and more are being created daily by computer programmers. You may not know all file types. I cannot tell you I know all file types, since that will surely be a white lie. This does not mean you cannot learn about file types. You have just learned basic files and their types. You have learned that a file can be malicious or a virus, even if it is a file you know, if infected—be careful!

TEST YOURSELF

1. What types of **Files** do you know?
2. What is a **Real File**?
3. What is a **Shortcut File Icon**?
4. What are **File Endings**?

CHAPTER 4: FOLDERS

Folders are directories or locations where you can store your information, such as files and other folders. Folders are also stored in another folder or directory, such as the hard drives. Your computer contains Windows with many other folders in the **C: Drive** by default.

The documents and other libraries in Windows 7 are examples of folders, where you can save your files. By default, a picture file is saved in the **picture library** and a document file is saved in the **document library** and so on. When you take a picture of yourself using your webcam, the file will be stored in the picture library folder. A folder or directory can only be opened, using a program that is part of Windows, and that program is called **Windows/File Explorer**.

Without this program, you cannot be able to do anything on your computer. The **Taskbar**, **Start Button** and all desktop icons will not be seen without **Windows/File Explorer**! If this program or this Windows feature is not running for whatever reasons, one cannot be able to open any directory on a computer, until the tool is back to normal.

Have you ever seen a message saying, "**Windows/File Explorer stopped working?**" What did you do to make it work again? In most cases, the program starts or restarts after crash. You cannot open any folder or directory, when the **Windows/File Explorer** is not running because all directories and folders only open in **Windows/File Explorer**. The Control Panel will not also open and this means you cannot fix your computer problems, if **Windows/File Explorer** crashed.

WINDOWS/FILE EXPLORER

Windows/File Explorer is a file management software, that we use to explore and open directories such as folders or drives including the computer folder, with all its drives and folders. You can open folders, using Explorer, and you can open directories, such as Control Panel, which is not really a folder but a set of instructions for your computer.

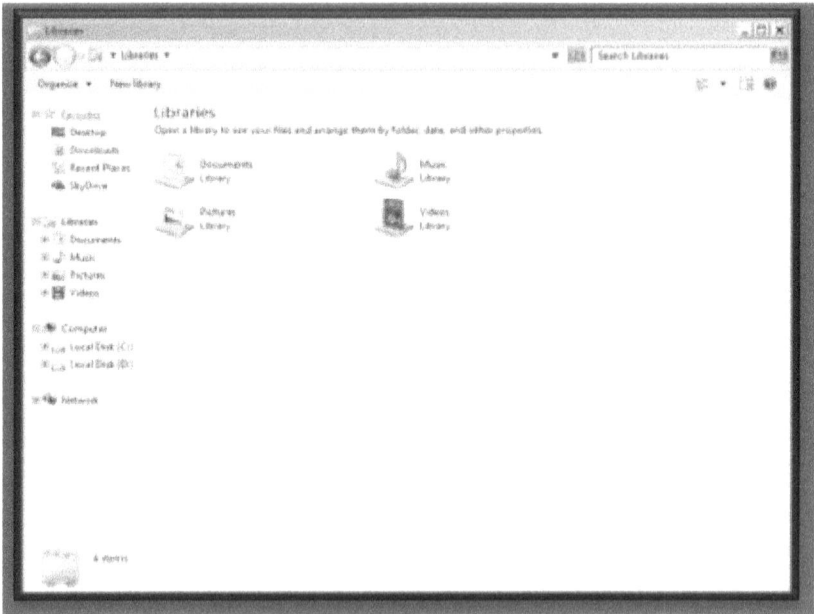

Figure 23: Windows/File Explorer

Windows/File Explorer is always pinned to your Taskbar in Windows Vista and in Windows 7 by default. Nevertheless, you can open it by opening any folder on the desktop or from the Start Menu discussed earlier. The folders like Documents, Music, Pictures, and Videos are located on the **C: drive** of your computer and you can explore them using **Windows/File Explorer**. Now, you can see how important **Windows/File Explorer** is.

We are going to discuss many things about folders shortly. There are many different parts of a folder and a folder is called window, which is exactly where we got the name for our Microsoft Operating System: Windows. We are learning about the seventh version of Windows Operating System, the most used software on many PCs today worldwide (before v10). After discussing the parts of a window, we will also look closely to the directory, which is another term for folders. Beware that technology terminology change from time to time.

FOLDER PARTS

A folder has many parts as mentioned above; but what are those parts? Do you want to know them right now? You are welcome. Remember, a folder is a container on a computer, where you keep your files.

In a folder, you can do many things with your files based on the settings you make, using folder options discussed earlier. Folder parts are very important to learn, because you can use them to work with your computer, and knowing more about them will really enhance your computing skills.

There are three main parts of a window that you have to know well. These parts are also called, control buttons. The **Minimize** button is one of them, followed by **Maximize/Restore Down** button. The last button on a window is **Close Button**.

These buttons always appear on the top-right corner of any opened window, but this also depends on the program you are running. Some programs do not have any control buttons, depending on the designing work of a program's maker—programmer.

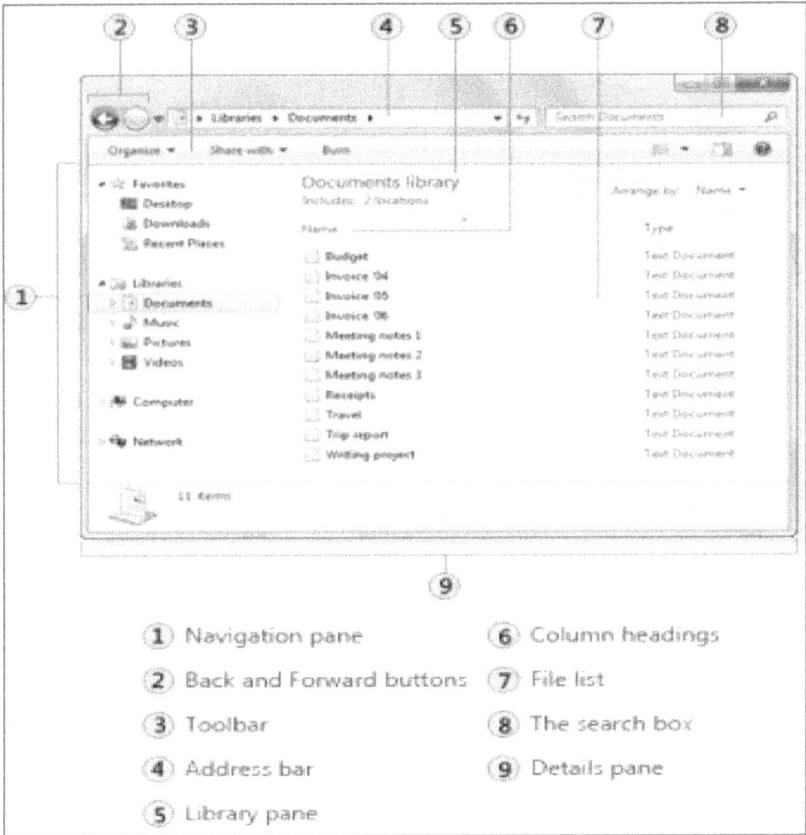

Figure 24: Library parts

Like any other window, a folder has a title bar where the name of that particular folder is displayed, and a menu bar, where you can find many other commands and tasks you can work with.

1. Navigation pane

This is part of a folder, where you can have access to files and other folders, even the entire hard disk drive on your computer. The navigation pane is located on the left side of the open folder. The navigation pane contains favourites, libraries, computer and network in Windows 7. However, it can contain different links depending on the Operating System you are currently using. The navigation pane is very important, because it helps you navigate.

2. Back and forward buttons

This is where you can navigate back to the previous location you recently opened, or you can go forward to where you were by using an arrow, pointing to the right. The forward arrow points to the right, while the backward arrow points to the left, and the buttons are located on the very top-left corner of any open folder window.

3. Toolbar

This is what I called menu bar, because it is a place where you can command the computer to do certain things in the current open folder. The toolbar can allow you to burn, share, organize or even create a new folder.

This is different in Windows XP, because in XP, you can find all of these links on the left side, which is now our navigation pane as discussed above. The toolbar contains tools and you can only see a few of these tools if you did not select an item in the folder.

If you select an item or items in the current open folder, other tools such as; 'e-mail' and 'open' commands will be added to the toolbar.

4. Address bar

This is the place where you can see the current folder and the location where you are in. You can use the address bar to go to a certain location or folder on your computer. However, you have to type the right location, using a forward slash (/).

For example the **Libraries/Documents**, will open the document libraries, if you type that in the address bar on the open folder.

Here you can type any file name stored on your computer and you may find it.

5. Library pane

This is a place where you can see the library type, for example, when you open the document library, the library pane will read **Documents** and now you know that you are in the document library. This appears when you are in a certain library.

6. Column headings

This is a place where you can see details of the current content of a folder, such as name and file type, including the size of the file. You can click on the heading to arrange how the name appears, and you can arrange from A-Z or backwards, that is Z-A.

7. File list

This shows you the list of files and other folders within the current opening folder. The file list is in the centre of the window/opened folder. If you type, a name of a certain file in the search box, the computer will display only the names in the current file list on the search results.

8. Search box

This is a place to type a word or phrase, and the computer will find that file for you, but the file must be on your computer or on a drive connected to your computer, in order for you to find it.

Nevertheless, most of the times, the file must be in the same folder where you are searching, so that you access it quickly. You can search for files or folders in this search box. This search box is just another version of the search box found on the Windows' Start Menu, because they all have the same functions.

9. Details pane

This pane tells you more about the contents of a folder, that is currently open, and if a file or files are selected, the details pane will indicate how many items are selected. It is the opposite to the title bar of an opened folder, because it is located at the very bottom of the folder window.

PARTS OF A WINDOW

A folder is a window, when opened, and we have discussed the most important parts of a folder above. However, we still have more to say about a window, because a folder is not really a window until it is open, and that is when it becomes a window.

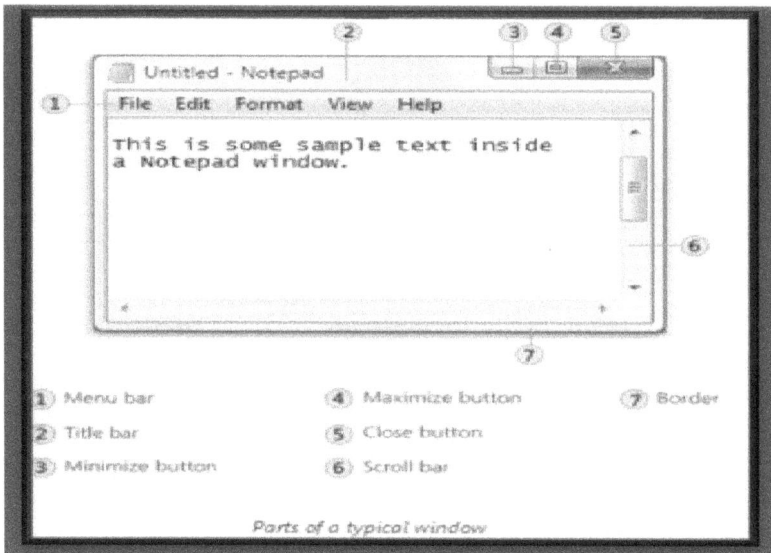

Figure 25: Window parts

In any open window, you can see the title bar, which also contains the control buttons on the top-right, such as minimize, restore down/maximize and close buttons. These buttons help you control the window, but you can also do more to the window in different ways.

You can resize the window or drag it to other locations on the desktop, by clicking and dragging while holding the left button mouse. You can resize any window by pointing and clicking on the edges and then drag to any direction. The direction to drag the window can be left, right, down, and up; but that window must be on the **Restore Down** position in order for you to resize it.

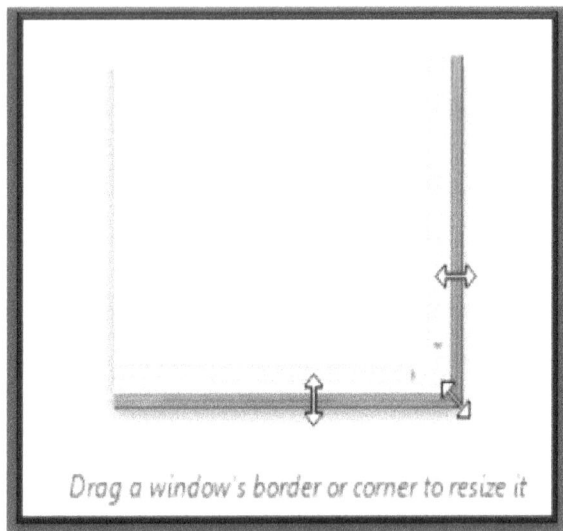

Drag a window's border or corner to resize it

Figure 26: Resize a window

If a window is in the maximize mode, you cannot change or resize it, because it is already covering the whole screen, but this also depends on the window you are working with. Some programs are designed not to be maximized by the user, and one example of such programs is my Windows Program Launcher.

To minimize a window is not the same as to close it, because to minimize a window means to place it into the Taskbar for quick access when needed. When a window is closed, you cannot be able to find it on the Taskbar when you need it. You have to look for the file and open it again. If you want to open the recently opened file, go to Start Button, and look for its program on the Start Menu.

Depending on your settings, you may find the link to your recently opened files and then open it again.

DIRECTORIES

The term **Directory** refers to a folder or location on a computer. Your computer folder is a directory or location where you can be able to view the current drives, such as USB, DVDs or CDs connected or inserted into your computer.

You can navigate easily to any directory through a window, or an open folder discussed above under folder parts. On the left of any folder that is opened, you can see the navigation pane, where you can have full access to drives and locations on your computer including the Control Panel.

Any place on your computer is a directory, including the computer folder. The External Hard Drive or any other storage media is a directory, when connected to your computer, because it becomes a storage space for your files.

Depending on your computer, you may have many or at least two partitions. A partition is a section of the Internal Hard Disk, that you can create, but you cannot create partitions using this beginner's guide, because the task is a bit advanced.

Even on my Microsoft Windows 7 with advanced features, I did not discuss how to create partitions. Creating partitions can make you lose your work, unless you are an expert on what you are doing.

On the coming pages, we will discuss directories, using a picture of the main folder. The main folder as shown below is a computer folder, and you can easily see the partitions I have on my computer, plus the external drive directory—DVD/CD-ROM.

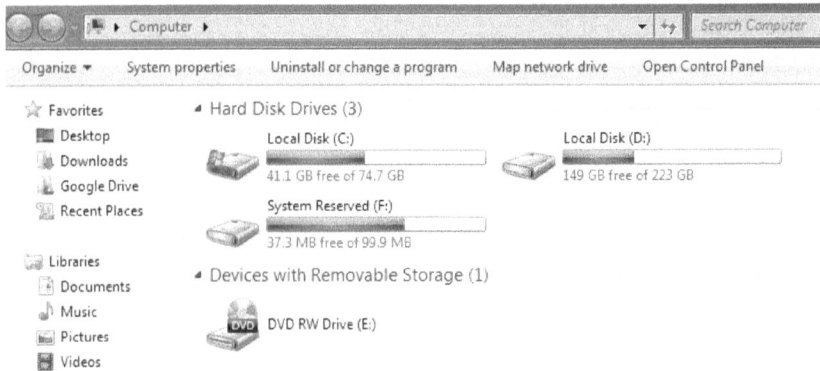

Figure 27: Drives

I assume you are an absolute beginner, and I do not allow you to dive into the world of computing by doing anything in the Control Panel in your Windows 7, because this book was written with beginners in mind. Windows 7 Control Panel is also available now (Part IV), and you may want to have it in order for you to do more with your computer. I hope this book (Part I) has helped you in many areas.

TEST YOURSELF

1. What is a **Folder?**
2. What is **Windows/File Explorer?**
3. What are **Folder Parts?**
4. Name some **Window Parts.**
5. What is a **Directory?**
6. Open your **Computer Folder.**

SUMMARY

This is Part I summary in simple words, which will make us understand everything discussed in the book. You have learned many things. You might have known all this information before. My goal is to make you understand common features of Windows 7, no matter what version you are running. You may be using Starter, Home Basic, Home Premium, Professional or even Ultimate.

The topic applies to all versions of Windows, and I believe everything discussed in this book will help you in many ways. In this simplified guide, you have learned about desktop items, such as Icons, wallpapers, Gadgets, Start Menu and the Taskbar. You have also explored the Start Button and its items such as the Search box, Start Menu, Commands, Links and All Programs. You have also learned about files and their types: real files and shortcut files. You have learned about file endings, also known as file name extensions, which helps you identify file types. You have learned about folders, Windows Explorer, parts of a folder, parts of a window and directories. These are important things you need to know about a computer as a beginner. I hope you enjoyed Part I.

BOOK 2: WINDOWS 7 CONTROL PANEL

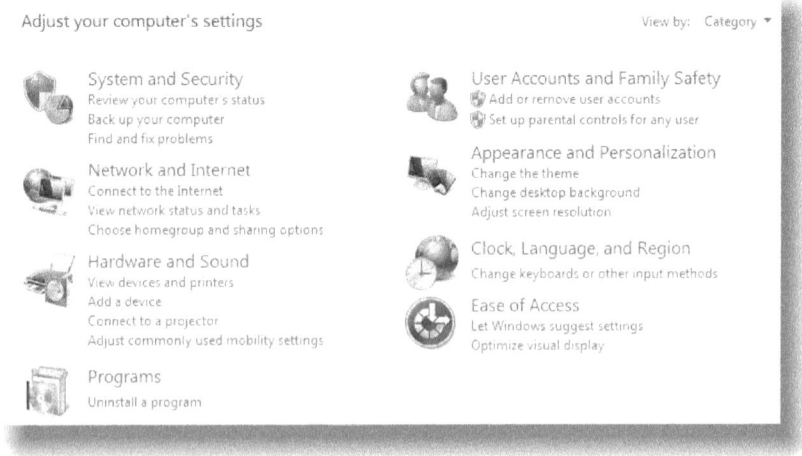

Adjust your computer's settings   View by: Category ▼

System and Security
Review your computer's status
Back up your computer
Find and fix problems

Network and Internet
Connect to the Internet
View network status and tasks
Choose homegroup and sharing options

Hardware and Sound
View devices and printers
Add a device
Connect to a projector
Adjust commonly used mobility settings

Programs
Uninstall a program

User Accounts and Family Safety
Add or remove user accounts
Set up parental controls for any user

Appearance and Personalization
Change the theme
Change desktop background
Adjust screen resolution

Clock, Language, and Region
Change keyboards or other input methods

Ease of Access
Let Windows suggest settings
Optimize visual display

Figure 28: Windows 7 Control Panel

INTRODUCTION TO WINDOWS 7 CONTROL PANEL

This part is a guide that will help you explore Windows 7 Control Panel feature in details. You need to put into practice each unit in this guide. First, I will help you find the Control Panel feature, and its tools. Then we will explore each tool at a time, based on the category the tool belongs. There are eight main categories in the Windows 7 Control Panel. We are going to learn how to use these categories in this section (Part IV).

The first category is known as *System and Security*. As the name suggests, this is where you will find and fix security related issues. The second category is, *Network and Internet*. This is where you will connect to the Internet, using wireless or wired connections, depending on what you have. The third feature is, *Hardware and Sound*. If your computer is having a sound problem, you may fix it from here. You can connect to the Internet here, or just view the Internet status and tasks. The fourth category is, *Programs*. This is where you can view all installed programs on your computer. If you decide you do not need a program, you can remove it from your system. The fifth category is, *User Accounts and Family Safety*. This is like the System and Security feature, because it helps protect your computer from hackers and malware. The sixth category is, *Appearance and Personalization*. Here, you can set the desktop background/wallpaper, system sounds, screen savers and more. The seventh category is *Clock, Language, and Region*. This is where you can set the date and time of your computer, including the time zone. The last category is, *Ease of Access*. We use this to make a computer usage easier for disabled people. Explore the tools and become a computer guru.

Windows 7 Control Panel is one main great tool in Windows Operating System. On Windows 7 Control Panel, I decided to go deeper to explain more about these tools and how you can use them. You can jump to any section of this section (Part IV), depending on your needs. See the introduction page for lessons discussed, so that you know where to go.

You must have the administrative rights on your computer, in order to have access to the Control Panel tools and features. If you are using a *Standard Account* or *Guest Account*, the system will not allow you to use many parts of Control Panel.

The access to some parts of the Control Panel depends on the User Account Control settings—(UAC). UAC settings, can only be changed by a system administrator—you. Indeed, this guide is meant for the advanced computer users like you. If you do not know anything or if you just know a little about computers, you have to be careful with the lessons given here in Part IV. If you make changes that will tamper with your system, the author will not be responsible in any way. You have to know what you are doing before you make any changes to your system. This is the main reason why this book is only meant for adults or people from 18 years of age and above.

The book does not have any organized tests but, in each chapter you can practice the lessons learned, if you need to use that particular feature to fix a problem. If you have a sound problem, use **Hardware and Sound** feature to fix it. You can read more about the author by searching the Amazon website. You will get his other books about computers. The units in the book are organized as they appear in the Control Panel section of Windows 7.

Control Panel's Main Window

How do you open the Control Panel window on your computer? If you have no idea how to do that, just follow these steps.

1. Click the **Start Button** on the bottom-left corner of the Windows screen.

2. Click the Control Panel link on the right side of the Start Menu, and you are done!

3. Change the view to your choice.

There are always three views, **category**, **small icons** and **large icons**. I personally like the category view, because it helps me find features I want very easily, compared to other views.

Now, let us explore the Control Panel. There are 8 main items on the Control Panel in Microsoft Windows 7. We are going to discuss each item in details. Once again, knowing these items and tools will help you control how your computer works for you. We will start with the main important feature, called "**System and Security**". As the name suggests, this is where you control your system and security.

Most computer users nowadays do not care whether they know something about their system or not. Some do not even know whether their antivirus programs work or not. When you ask them, they say they are not **computer wizards** or **professionals**. They do not know much about computers. The truth is if you are using a machine, you must know what to do with it. I want you to know how to fix your computer problems after reading this book. This is the heart of my writings—helping you fix problems.

You will learn how to uninstall programs, which you do not really need. You will learn how to find and fix different common computer errors, yourself. When your computer cannot respond, what can you do? You can force it to shut down and restart it, if it cannot turn off normally.

You will learn how to personalize your desktop background, including the setting of the screen saver and much more. If you found out that you know all these things, feel free to use the book in teaching others who may not know these things. Explore the eight items of Control Panel and learn how you can use these tools to fix common computer problems, yourself. Take your computer to IT personnel only when you cannot resolve a problem. Most problems can be resolved without an IT personnel's help.

What is the relationship between my views and computing? Well, the reality is I teach you what I do, not what I was taught in school. Since I learned all these tips through practice, I also want you to believe you can do the same. It is my belief that my readers can do more than I do. This is the reason I write computer manuals.

You may also like reading more on my blog about computers and faith. If you really believe what I say, you will explore even more on the Control Panel, and you will love the book. Be careful not to do something that you do not understand!

CHAPTER 1: SYSTEM AND SECURITY

~~**~~

Action Center
Review your computer's status and resolve issues | Change User Account Control settings
Troubleshoot common computer problems | Restore your computer to an earlier time

Windows Firewall
Check firewall status | Allow a program through Windows Firewall

System
View amount of RAM and processor speed | Check the Windows Experience Index
Allow remote access | See the name of this computer | Device Manager

Windows Update
Turn automatic updating on or off | Check for updates | View installed updates

Power Options
Change battery settings | Require a password when the computer wakes
Change what the power buttons do | Change when the computer sleeps

Backup and Restore
Back up your computer | Restore files from backup

Administrative Tools
Free up disk space | Defragment your hard drive | Create and format hard disk partitions
View event logs | Schedule tasks

Figure 29: System and Security

This is the feature discussed earlier in the book. What I am going to do here is showing you how to access this feature, and the reason why you have to access it. Under **System and Security**, you can find security related tools and most of these tools have been mentioned earlier.

Action Centre—this is where you can review your computer's status, then and resolve common issues, troubleshoot common computer problems, and deal with other different security related issues. You can even change the User Account Controls settings here. You can restore your computer to an earlier time and condition, right here.

HOW DO I DO THIS?

Click the Action Centre icon to access the tools and options in the Control Panel. The Action Centre window will look like the one shown below. Make sure the title bar of the window reads, "**Action Centre**," with a flag-like icon. The Action Centre in Windows XP is called **Windows Security Centre**.

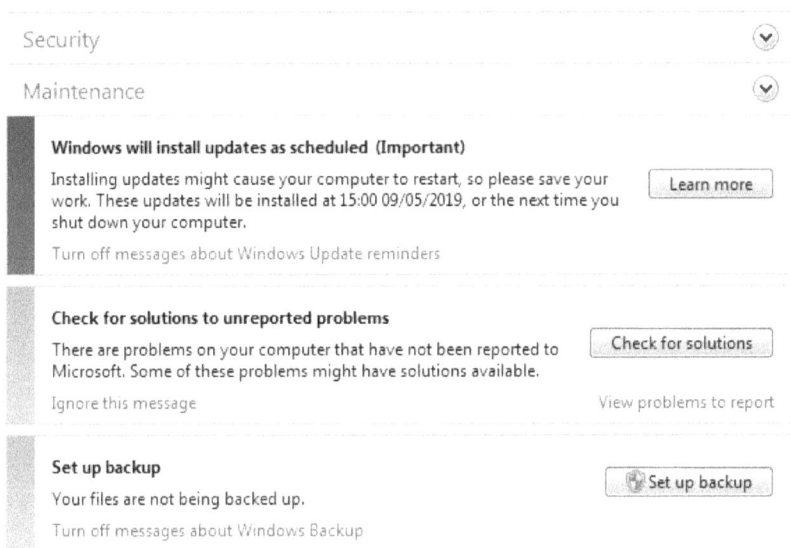

Security

Maintenance

Windows will install updates as scheduled (Important)
Installing updates might cause your computer to restart, so please save your work. These updates will be installed at 15:00 09/05/2019, or the next time you shut down your computer.

Learn more

Turn off messages about Windows Update reminders

Check for solutions to unreported problems
There are problems on your computer that have not been reported to Microsoft. Some of these problems might have solutions available.

Check for solutions

Ignore this message   View problems to report

Set up backup
Your files are not being backed up.

Set up backup

Turn off messages about Windows Backup

Figure 30: Action Centre

In addition, it is where you can find and fix many security issues. You will find and fix security related problems, such as issues to do with your antivirus software or Windows Firewall. You can also find and fix issues to do with computer maintenance, such as error reporting or backup issues.

The Action Centre reports problems in the notification area for you to take an action as soon as possible, depending on what the problem is. If the problem has a yellow colour icon, it means it is not very serious. Yet, you have to pay attention to it. You have to fix the problem and Windows will always show you how to fix it.

Some issues have to be reported to Microsoft. To report an issue, just click a button that says **Report Issues**. You can also read more about what to report to Microsoft. Be sure the software that is running or sending reports is a Microsoft-built, not a third-party tool for security reasons. Some programs pretend to be from Microsoft, they can steal your passwords, and usernames after you run them on your system!

The above picture shows that I have one problem with **Maintenance**, but no security issue reported. My problem as seen above is about checking for solutions to unreported problems. I can then view the problems to report or ignore this message by clicking the right button for each action as shown above in the picture. Under **Security** tab, I can resolve issues related to my antivirus program or my Windows Firewall.

Now, let me expand the maintenance window for us to see more actions. An alert with a red colour icon is very important, meaning you have to take action as soon as possible. The alert with yellow colour like the one shown above is not very serious, but you had better fix it or it will get serous in the near future. If you do not backup your computer and files, and anything unexpected happen to the machine, you will lose all your work.

Windows can help you find and fix these problems easily if you agree to do so, using **Action Centre** on the Control Panel, and this is the reason I wrote this book. As you can see in the picture above, I can now check for solutions to problems reported or unreported. In my case, this option is turned on. The actions under this area are for me to check for solutions, view the privacy policy for checking solutions, go to settings, or view the reliability history of my computer. The next thing here is backup, which in my case is currently not monitored, meaning the computer cannot alert me about backup.

You can then turn on messages about Windows backup, if you want to do so, in case you have the same settings like mine. Windows Backup messages are turned on by default, but you can turn them off, if you do not need them. However, Windows Backup feature helps you in maintenance, so that if anything happens to your computer, you will not lose your work, if it was backed up on an External Hard Disk.

Use this tool, because it is important. The other item is about checking for Windows Updates. In my case, no action is required, because my computer checks for updates automatically, every day I connected it to the Internet. The other item in the list is troubleshooting system maintenance. In my case, no action needed, because I have set my computer to alert me about system maintenance.

However, you can change the troubleshooting settings to suit your needs, using the link that says, **"Change troubleshooting settings"** shown in the picture above. There are still many links, such as change Action Centre settings, Change User Account Control settings, view archived messages and view performance information, all on the far top-left of the activity centre window, shown above.

On the bottom-left corner of the Action Centre window, you can see the links, such as Backup and Restore, Windows Update and Windows Program Compatibility Troubleshooter. You can click these links for more actions needed. If there are no problems, Action Centre will look clean. Action Centre is very important, because it is where a computer tells you what to do, regarding the security and maintenance. As you can see, you can fix most problems, yourself here. You do not really have to have a degree in computers in order for you to do this.

You do not have to be a mathematician to know what 5 x 10 is and this is the same with fixing your computer issues, and common problems. All you need is a manual like this, and you can practice what you learned.

Help protect your computer with Windows Firewall

Windows Firewall can help prevent hackers or malicious software from gaining access to your computer through the Internet or a network.

How does a firewall help protect my computer?

What are network locations?

| Home or work (private) networks | Not Connected ⊗ |
| Public networks | Connected ⊗ |

Figure 31: Windows Firewall

Windows Firewall—this is where you can check firewall status, and allow a program through a firewall. Make sure you know the program you want to allow through the Windows firewall because that can tamper with your security.

You can easily get infected if you allow malicious software through a firewall. The firewall is your computer's shield, because it protects it from attacks from the network. It is not an antivirus, but it is a barrier for viruses. It blocks programs that may invite viruses to your system, until you choose to enable them.

Do not enable a program through the firewall, unless you know the program and the company that makes it. Knowing the name of the program and the company is not enough. I once installed a program, called **Fix It**, which messed up my system! The software claimed to be an antivirus, while it was a virus by itself.

On the Firewall window above, you can do many things. You can allow a program feature or through Windows Firewall, you can change the notification settings, and you can turn off/on the Windows Firewall.

You can even restore default settings of Windows Firewall, or go to the advanced settings or troubleshoot your network. To learn more about firewall, just click the link that reads, "How does a firewall help protect my computer?" You can also learn more about network locations. The best thing about the computer is that it is a teacher of itself. All you can do is to read and understand what it says, and you are done.

There is home or work network in the network location. There are also public networks. My firewall state is **ON**, meaning it is turned on to help protect my computer. My incoming connection is set to block all connections to programs that are not on the list of allowed programs, and you should set yours this way for security reasons.

You can see active public networks if any are active now. You can also see **Action Centre** window here by using links on the bottom-left corner of the firewall window. There is also a link there to the network and sharing centre.

View basic information about your computer

Windows edition

Windows 7 Professional

Copyright © 2009 Microsoft Corporation. All rights reserved.

System

Rating:	**4.4** Windows Experience Index
Processor:	Intel(R) Celeron(R) CPU B820 @ 1.70GHz 1.70 GHz
Installed memory (RAM):	2.00 GB (1.78 GB usable)
System type:	32-bit Operating System
Pen and Touch:	No Pen or Touch Input is available for this Display

Figure 32: System Information

System—this is a place where you can view the amount of RAM and processor speed on your machine, allow remote access to your computer over the Internet, see the name of your computer, check Windows Experience Index and open the Device Manager. You have a full control as a system administrator, and you can make almost any change you want to your computer here.

Here, I can see basic information about my computer. I can see the edition of Windows 7, and in my case, it is Windows 7 Professional. My service Pack is 1, and this is the version number. Service packs can be downloaded manually from Microsoft Website free. However, your system will download and install the latest service pack, depending on the Windows Update settings. My system manufacturer is Toshiba, and the model of this computer is Satellite L455. The Windows Experience Index rate is 3.3.

This feature allows the Microsoft tools to determine the performance of my computer. My processor is Intel® Celeron® CPU 900 © 2.20GHz, 2.19 GHz. My installed RAM or Random Access Memory is 2.00 GB (1.87 GB usable). My system type is

Win32, meaning it is a 32 bit operating system. This is very important to know, especially when I want to install new programs that may not work on win32 system. You can see that I have no pen or touch screen. Some computers have those features. On my System window, I can go to device manager, remote settings, system protection and advanced system settings. These links are found on the top-left corner of the system window in the Control Panel feature of Windows 7. Toshiba support is on the website, and the link to the website is given in the window on the picture above.

Windows activation

Windows is activated

Product ID: 00371-OEM-8992671-00013

Learn more online...

Figure 33: Genuine Windows

On the picture above, you can see more details about your computer. For now, I can see my computer's domain name and Workgroup settings. I can also see that my Windows is activated, and it reads, **Genuine** on the far bottom-right of the System window screen as shown above in the picture. If my Windows version was not activated, I can see more options, such as activate Windows online, and other things.

I hope your system is also activated. You can learn more online about what it means to activate your Windows version by clicking, "Learn more online link…" Many computer gurus use programs to crack the Windows Activation Technology (WAT).

Do not try to use those tools, because most of them come with viruses, that can harm your system more than what you can imagine! The other links you may need to use are on the bottom-left corner of the System window, such as Action Centre, Windows Update and Performance Information and Tools.

Your product ID is unique, meaning you can use it only on your computer—genuine Windows. What if your Windows software is not genuine for whatever reasons? It is true that people buy computers with Windows loaded on them from the market, and then after a few days or weeks, they begin to experience system issues. I suggest you go back to your seller, and ask for more advice on what to do. In South Sudan, people are selling free antivirus programs to people who know nothing about computers, and they get money for that!

As mentioned earlier, people also crack Windows and resell copies to those who need them, and this is a serious crime especially in the West—US. Do not crack Windows, because this will harm you or your system, whether you know it or not. These hackers hack you before they hack anything else, so beware!

Someone may ask you to download and install a crack tool, because your Windows is not genuine, and you cannot purchase the right copy online for whatever reasons. One reason for you not to purchase Windows online maybe is that you do not have a credit card. The other reason can be not having enough money to purchase the software, and you need one. Whatever the case, I understand you need Windows. Nevertheless, as an experienced person in the so called Windows Activation cracks or Windows 7 loader, my advice for you is do not to use these tools. These tools will expose you to hackers.

Figure 34: Windows Update

Windows Update—you can now turn on/off the automatic Windows Update here. You can check for updates manually, and view the installed Windows updates. We have discussed the importance of this Windows feature in previous chapters.

As you can see in the picture above, the system is asking me to check for the updates now. It says, "Always install the latest updates to enhance your computer's security and performance" and then there is a button, "**Install updates**," on the far right.

Below that dialogue box, there are things like, "Most recent check for updates, Updates was installed, and you receive updates." I can even view, update history here. On the far left, I can check for updates, change the Windows Update settings, view, update history, and restore hidden updates.

I can even view Updates frequently asked questions, using Windows Help and Support feature. I can also view the installed updates, using the link at the bottom-left corner of Windows Update window as shown above. Remember, updates will cause problems in your system, if you are running pirated Windows. Make sure your copy of Windows is genuine.

Select a power plan

Power plans can help you maximize your computer's performance or conserve energy. Make a plan active by selecting it, or choose a plan and customize it by changing its power settings. Tell me more about power plans

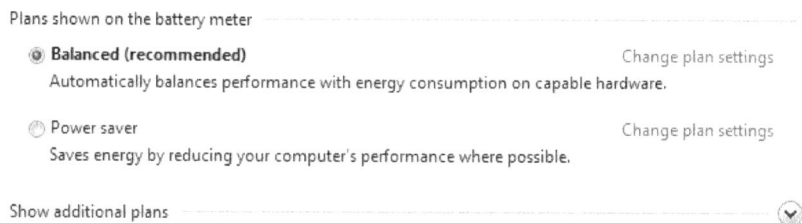

Plans shown on the battery meter

◉ **Balanced (recommended)**   Change plan settings
    Automatically balances performance with energy consumption on capable hardware.

◎ Power saver   Change plan settings
    Saves energy by reducing your computer's performance where possible.

Show additional plans   ⌄

Figure 35: Power Options

Power options—you may realize that some features have been discussed earlier, and we are repeating them here. Under power option feature, you can change the battery settings, change what the power buttons do, require a password when your computer wakes up from sleep, and change when the computer sleeps, all under this feature. Depending on your computer, there can be different power plans. In the above picture, you can see that I have two power plans. The balanced power plan is selected, meaning that is a plan I was using when I wrote this manual.

You can change the power plan settings by clicking the link for changing the settings, and follow the on-screen instructions on how to do this. The easy way to get into a power plan window is clicking the Start Button and type **Power**. You can then click the power options link and you will be there. On the picture above, you can choose to show additional plans or create your own. On the top-left corner of the window, you can find other useful links such as: require a password on wakeup, choose what the power button does, create a power plan, choose when to turn off display, and change when the computer sleeps.

You can also find links to Personalization, Windows Mobility Centre and User Account, on the bottom-left corner of the power options window as shown above. You may also want to reduce or increase the screen brightness by using the slide that you can see at the bottom-centre of the window above.

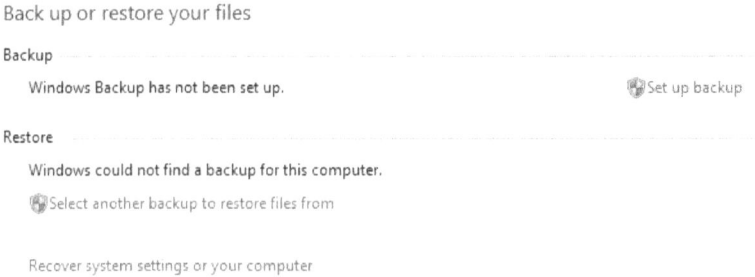

Back up or restore your files

Backup

Windows Backup has not been set up.   Set up backup

Restore

Windows could not find a backup for this computer.

Select another backup to restore files from

Recover system settings or your computer

Figure 36: Backup and Restore

Backup and Restore—you can backup your entire computer from here, or restore the system or Windows from a backup. You can restore files or the whole Windows system from the backup on a CD, DVD or any other storage media, in case anything happens to the computer in the future.

Backup and Restore feature can allow you to do many other good things on your computer. It can allow you to restore the system to the earlier state, could anything happen to the system. If your computer was running fine yesterday, and then today in the morning hours, but at noon it had a problem. You then tried to restart it and it is not responding. In the process, it could not even boot or start as normal. The System Restore can be the first best option after this. You can now try the System Restore, which does not work with all systems and computers, but you can set it up for your computer.

Now, you can click the, "**Set up backup**," link to set up a new backup. This feature in Windows is good for maintenance, because if you backup your important files, they will be safe if anything happened to your computer.

You can select another backup to restore files from. The backup devices can be **External Hard disks** or **DVDs** and **CDs**. You can restore your system settings of your computer here. On the top-left corner of the **Backup and Restore** window, you can find links such as, create a system image, and create a system repair disc, and these are two different things.

There are also links to the Action Centre, and Windows Easy Transfer. The Windows Easy Transfer helps you transfer files from an old computer to the new one very easily, but you have to follow some steps to do this. The Windows Backup window will look like the one below when you click the setup backup link.

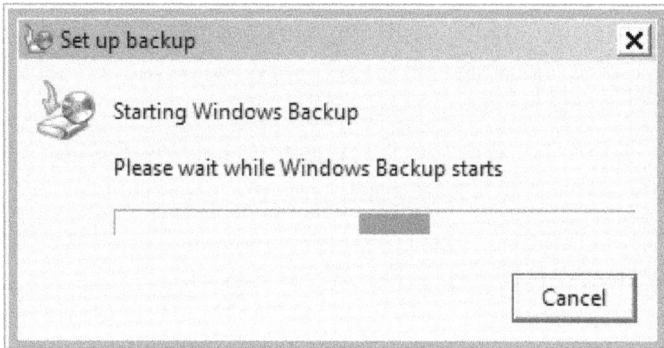

Figure 37: Backup process

You cannot setup a backup on a drive on the same hard disk drive of your computer. For this reason, you will be asked to use an external disk, when you set up a backup. The System Restore could not be interrupted, please use this when you are sure you really want to restore your system after a serious problem. The system image can be created, using a link on the top-left hand side of the **Backup and Restore** window shown above. You can create a system image to be used in the future, in case your computer stopped working for whatever reasons.

The system image is the whole computer image/copy, meaning the whole operating system will be backed up. This may take few **DVDs** and many **CDs**, depending on the size of your hard disk and the programs on it. The system repair disc can be used to repair your computer, if it refused to restart because of a problem.

Computers have many different problems, and it is recommended you create a system repair disk as soon as possible, when you buy a new computer. When your computer could not start for whatever reasons, you can use your system repair disc now, to restore the machine to the earlier state, but your files may not be deleted. System restore is the best feature I personally use to repair computers. It is the first action I take, when a computer encountered any serious problem. It is not true that all computers will have this feature enabled. I encourage you to enable this feature as soon as possible, by clicking the create system restore point. You can do this on the system protection feature, or when you are installing any new third-party software such as Advanced SystemCare. Microsoft Security Essentials also have an option for creating a system restore, under the settings tab.

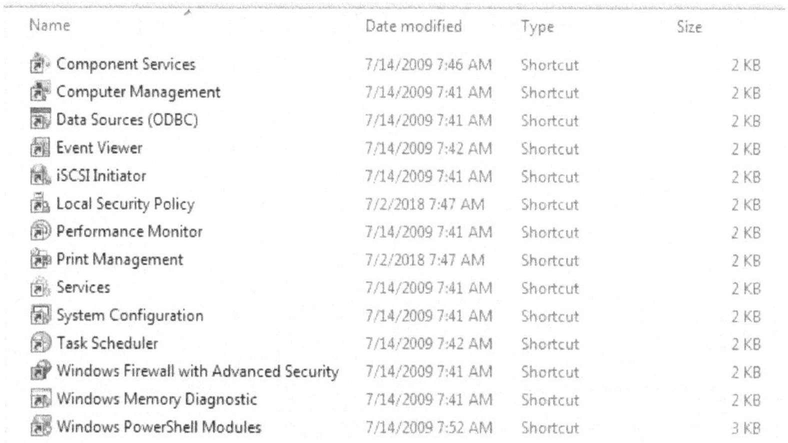

Name	Date modified	Type	Size
Component Services	7/14/2009 7:46 AM	Shortcut	2 KB
Computer Management	7/14/2009 7:41 AM	Shortcut	2 KB
Data Sources (ODBC)	7/14/2009 7:41 AM	Shortcut	2 KB
Event Viewer	7/14/2009 7:42 AM	Shortcut	2 KB
iSCSI Initiator	7/14/2009 7:41 AM	Shortcut	2 KB
Local Security Policy	7/2/2018 7:47 AM	Shortcut	2 KB
Performance Monitor	7/14/2009 7:41 AM	Shortcut	2 KB
Print Management	7/2/2018 7:47 AM	Shortcut	2 KB
Services	7/14/2009 7:41 AM	Shortcut	2 KB
System Configuration	7/14/2009 7:41 AM	Shortcut	2 KB
Task Scheduler	7/14/2009 7:42 AM	Shortcut	2 KB
Windows Firewall with Advanced Security	7/14/2009 7:41 AM	Shortcut	2 KB
Windows Memory Diagnostic	7/14/2009 7:41 AM	Shortcut	2 KB
Windows PowerShell Modules	7/14/2009 7:52 AM	Shortcut	3 KB

Figure 38: Administrative Tools

Administrative Tools—you can free the disk space here, view event logs, defragment your hard drives, schedule tasks, and create and format hard disk partitions on your computer. You remember our disk clean up and disk defragmenter? This is where you can get the tools for use on your computer, if you need them.

There are many tools you can use in this feature, and we are not going to explain everything about each tool. You can see these tools with shortcut file type, meaning these are not real files but shortcuts to the Control Panel real files. You can see the Component Services, Computer Management, Data Sources (ODBC), and Event Viewer, iSCSI Initiator, Local Security Policy, Performance Monitor. You can even see the Print Management, Services, System Configuration, Task Scheduler, and Windows Firewall with Advanced Security on Local Computer, Windows Memory Diagnostic and finally, the Windows Powershell Modules. You have to click twice and quickly (double-click) on the item that you want to open, and it will open. You may need to type your administrator password, when asked to do so by the system in order for you to access these critical areas on your computer. Please, make sure you know what you are doing with the tools, or else you will do something unexpected with your computer.

As mentioned earlier, some of these tools are very dangerous to use unless you know what you are going to do with them. The good thing is that, if you set your UAC well, you will be asked to provide an administrative password, whenever you try to modify anything important.

The System Configuration is one of the tools you do not have to use, unless you know what you are doing, because here, you can configure how your computer works. You can configure how the system will boot or start. The performance monitor is best for you to monitor the performance of your computer.

This means it is not all tools that are not good to use. But, as an advanced computer user, you are expected to try and learn these features. Remember, as you learn, you must also make mistakes, whether you like it or not, because it is natural to make mistakes. I make mistakes every time when I want to do something with my computer and this leads to finding solutions to problems.

I can now fix many computer issues, because I have made the same mistakes myself before, and I have learned how to get things back to normal. Never fear to learn, even though you may make mistakes in the end. Many people just want to know a little bit about computer. Some say they do not want to master computers, because this is not their area of service.

If you do not love to use a computer, then this book is not for you. You can use a computer in your ministry, no matter what ministry. If you are a pastor, you need a computer to type your sermons, and many other important documents. If you are a student, you need a computer for typing your assignments and other required academic papers. But, typing an assignment or document is not the only thing you can do with your computer.

Each university has some requirements for doing an assignment. For you to complete your assignment exactly as required by the university, you need some basic computing skills. However, as the sub-title of this book explained, this book assumes you are a system administrator. To be a system administrator does not mean you are employed in a computer work by an organization.

You can be a system administrator of your own computer just as I do. You need to be informed of the features of the System and Security section of your Windows Operating software, so that you can do something when needed. You are the administrator of your computer, because you fix security and maintenance issues, when needed. The computer maintenance can cost you money, but now you can do what you can and leave only what you cannot do to the IT personnel.

CHAPTER 2: NETWORK AND INTERNET

~~**~~

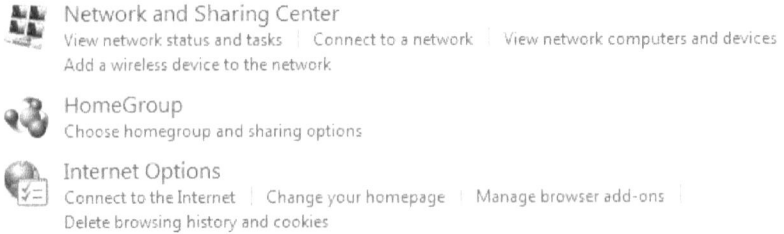

Network and Sharing Center
View network status and tasks | Connect to a network | View network computers and devices
Add a wireless device to the network

HomeGroup
Choose homegroup and sharing options

Internet Options
Connect to the Internet | Change your homepage | Manage browser add-ons
Delete browsing history and cookies

Figure 39: Network and Internet

Network and Sharing—this is where you can get connected to the internet. You can view the network status, and tasks, add a wireless device to the network, and connect to a network, and then view computers and devices on a network.

As you can see in the above picture, a computer called JOHN-PC (This computer) was connected to ECC GOLI GENERIC (Old version, now removed) and you can see the Internet icon there on the window. Here, I can set up a new connection or network, I can connect to a network, I can choose a HomeGroup and sharing options, or troubleshoot my internet connection problems. I can also manage wireless networks on my computer, whether my computer is connected to those networks or not, using a link on the top-left corner of **Network and Internet** window as shown above. I can also change the adapter settings or the advanced sharing settings in the same area. I can connect or disconnect from wireless networks in range. In addition, I can view HomeGroup, Internet Options, and Windows Firewall, using the links on the bottom-left corner of the window as shown in the picture above.

HomeGroup—you can choose home group and sharing options here under this feature.

I cannot use this feature because my computer must use the home group network, in order for me to use it. I can choose this option, when setting up my computer for the first time, or when installing my Windows (See Installing Windows 7 in Microsoft Windows 7 textbook). To learn more about this feature, simply click the right links provided. You can use links such as, "Tell me more about home groups," and you can change the advanced sharing settings, or start the HomeGroup troubleshooter from here. You can click, "Create a HomeGroup," icon when it is possible and follow the instructions for your machine.

Internet and Options—you can change your homepage here, manage your browser add-ons, and even delete your browsing history and cookies, but only on Windows Internet Explorer. For other Internet browsers, check them out, because they also have their settings that are not listed under Windows settings. The hardware and sound are one important feature for a computer's advanced user like you to know.

The Windows Internet Explorer has many tabs for many different settings, which we are not going to discuss here. Under the general tab above, you can change the homepage for your computer or use the default settings. There are many other tabs with different settings such as; security, privacy, content, connections, programs and advanced tabs.

You can also set the startup options of your browser by choosing the options such as; start with tabs from the last session, or start with a home page. You can change how web pages are displayed in tabs by clicking the tab button. You can choose to delete the browsing history by using the check mark next to delete browsing history on exit, or you can use the delete button.

You can also set this using the setting button as shown on the picture above. You can also change the appearance of your Internet Explorer, such as colour, using the colour button. You can set the languages and fonts and the accessibility, using the right buttons on the program window as shown above. After making your changes, click the **Ok** button to save your changes. You can cancel the settings or apply the settings using the right buttons on the program window as shown. Remember, these settings only apply to Internet Explorer, also known as Windows Internet Explorer, and these may not work with another browser, such as the Google Chrome, Firefox, or Opera. The Internet Explorer is the safest browser, but it is also slow compared to Firefox and Google Chrome.

The Network and Security feature in Windows 7 is where you can manage how you communicate with the world. It is the communication section of Windows. It is the place that can allow you to use the Internet and other network services, such as social network sites like Facebook, Twitter and more. When connected to the Internet or any other network, you can use Skype and other communication tools, such as e-mail from Yahoo! Google and more to communicate with people you know. For this reason, Network and Internet feature is very important for you to explore. I could not explain everything in this guide either, but I hope you have been helped.

If you already know how to connect to the Internet, praise God. You can now use your book as a manual to teach others, if you want to do so, especially if you are a teacher, and you love teaching others. It is my desire to see you learn how to connect to the Internet. Another thing about the Internet is that your network may have a password, and you have to know that password, before you could get connected. You can ask your network administrator to give you the password for the Internet, also known as network key. System administrators for security purposes use passwords, even though some folks can still steal information from computers, using modern technology. If you are a system administrator, then you know what I'm talking about.

CHAPTER 3: HARDWARE AND SOUND

~~**~~

Figure 40: Hardware and Sound

Hardware and Sound is a feature where you can set or even change hardware and sound settings in Windows. This feature allows you to make many good changes to your hardware and sound. As usual, you must have the administrative rights in order for you to use features in the Control Panel.

There are many links and commands to run under Hardware and Sound feature. The main items under this are, Devices and Printers, AutoPlay, Sound, Power Options, Display and Windows Mobility Centre.

◢ Devices (2)

ABIEL-PC   USB OPTICAL
                  MOUSE

◢ Printers and Faxes (4)

Fax   Microsoft XPS   Print To PDF   Send To
             Document Writer   (Copy 1)   OneNote 2007

Figure 41: Devices and Printers

Devices and printers—you can add a device, add a printer, change mouse settings, and run device manager. Windows normally adds new devices as soon as you connect them to the computer, but you can also use this feature to add a device to the computer, such as a printer, manually. Devices can be computer peripherals, or other tools you can use with your computer, such as USB or flash disks. The printers are output devices, used to print out documents or pictures from your computer.

You can do many things under this feature, using links given in the feature as shown in the above picture. We are going to look at the devices and printers now.

The first icons under devices are ABIEL-PC and USB OPTICAL MOUSE devices, but you may have more than what you can see here, depending on your computer. Below that under the printers and faxes you can see items (icons). These are; Fax, Windows XPS Document Writer and Send To OneNote 2007.

These are icons for various printers. Some of these printers will only convert a document or picture into a different format such as the XPS Writer and Print To PDF. The "Send to OneNote" printer will also convert a document into OneNote type or format. You may need to install more printer drivers on your computer. Some printing devices are not free, but you may get some free for your computer on the manufacturer's website. HP is one of the companies that can provide you with free drivers for HP printers. You also need to update your printer drivers, using the Windows Update feature in Windows. The best way to do this is to enable the automatic update, so that it downloads and install the right drivers for any program.

You may also need to view updates before you install them, because not all the updates are important for you. Some programs slow down your computer's performance, such as Bing Desktop or Google Desktop—the last item is not an update. We will discuss more on programs' chapter. Nevertheless, for now, you have learned there are many types of drivers and printers that you can install. One drive is your computer Hard Disk, but any connected device such as an External Hard Disk will appear under the devices and printers section of your windows. Any installed printer or fax driver will show up under **printers and faxes**.

A mouse can be one of your installed devices, if you are using an external mouse device, especially if you are using a laptop computer (It is not necessary to use a mouse on laptops). Now, you can check your computer to find out more about your devices and printers. You can troubleshoot or remove any device, if you want to. To troubleshoot a device or printer, click on it in the devices and printers window, and then choose **troubleshoot** action on the toolbar. Alternatively, you can right click the device and then choose **troubleshoot** action in the drop-down menu that will appear. You only troubleshoot devices that are not working properly for whatever reason (s). One reason for a device not to work properly is being out of date. If you do not update your computer from time to time, drivers will be out of date. As usual, you can update almost all drivers from Windows Update, but you have to setup Windows Update first. The automatic update is recommended. You can also use a driver itself to look for updates for that particular printer updates or that program. Each program has its unique ways to check for updates, or you can visit a vendor's website for help. Opening the device window can give you more options, including how to get help on updates. Some devices will lead you to the company's website for more help and support tools.

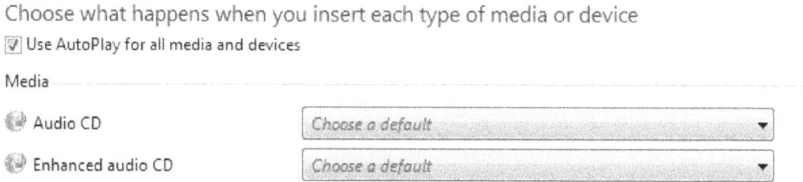

Choose what happens when you insert each type of media or device

☑ Use AutoPlay for all media and devices

Media

🖸 Audio CD   Choose a default   ▾

🖸 Enhanced audio CD   Choose a default   ▾

Figure 42: AutoPlay Settings

AutoPlay—you can change the default settings for audio, devices, to play CDs or other media, automatically. This setting may expose your computer to malware and other malicious programs. I suggest you turn it off. The AutoPlay is a feature that makes your computer opens the disc or any connected hard drive or memory stick, automatically. You can always change the settings. You can change the settings for CDs, DVDs and software games. You can set a default program to run a certain file type from a connected drive, or you can set the system to ask you first, every time. You can choose what your computer will do when you insert different types of media such as empty CDs, DVDs, Audio files, Video files and more. Click on the arrow next to the option, and then choose an action from the drop-down menu that will appear, and then save your settings. I personally do not use AutoPlay, because of security reasons. You may use third-party software, to stop your computer from opening drives connected to it automatically, using the auto play feature. I recommend IObit Advanced SystemCare for this, and you can search the Internet to get the tool, or find it here at www.iobit.com and choose the product, because there are many tools there for different devices.

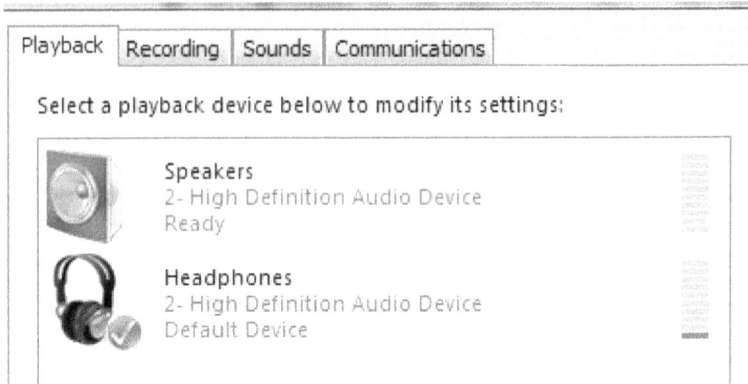

Figure 43: Sound Settings

Sound—you can adjust system volume, change system sounds, and manage audio and devices. There are many ways to access this feature, but the easy way is to go through the Control Panel as we are now explaining. As you can see on the above picture, you can do many things with the sound feature. There are four different tabs here. We are going to explore them now. The first one is shown above—**Playback**. You may have different software for the sound driver. Mine is *High Definition Audio Device*. The other tab is called **Recording**. Here, you can see the same device name, but with a different icon for recording sound.

I can use this device to record sound, but I must connect a headphone with my computer for me to do this. The sounds tab can allow me to choose the sound type I want for my computer, and there are many sounds by default. The communication tab shown above can allow me to do many other things such as mute all other sounds, reduce the volume of other sounds by 80% or 50% when playing this sound. I can choose the do nothing option—phone calls. Only one radio button can be used once at a time as shown above. I like using the "reduce volume" of other sound by 80% option and that is why I used it.

Power options—again, you can access the power options under this feature in Windows 7. You can now change the battery settings, require a password when computer wakes, if needed. Adjust the screen brightness, change what the power buttons do, and change when the computer sleeps. In the power option setting, please see the previous chapters.

Make it easier to read what's on your screen

You can change the size of text and other items on your screen by choosing one of these options. To temporarily enlarge just part of the screen, use the Magnifier tool.

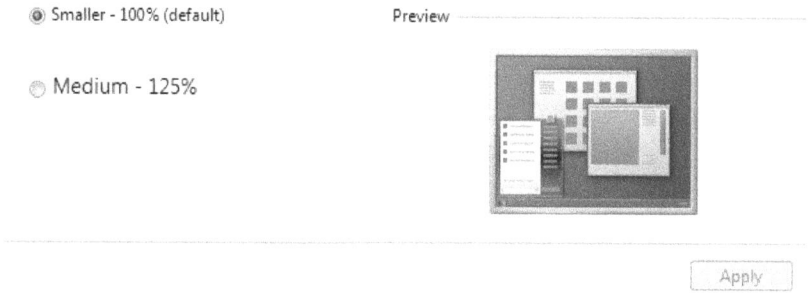

⦿ Smaller - 100% (default)   Preview

⦿ Medium - 125%

Apply

Figure 44: Display Settings

Display—you can make text and other items larger or smaller, connect to an external display, adjust the screen resolution or connect to a projector from here. There are many different processes to open the tool or feature in Windows. This is why I repeated some features. There are two radio buttons for the display setup as shown in the picture above. However, computers are not the same. Yours may differ from this. The first option is called "**Smaller,**" that is 100% (default), and you can see the preview for this setting on the far right hand side of the screen. The second item is called, "**Medium,**" and it is 125%, which means the resolution of your screen will be set to 125, if selected. The default screen setting is 100%/**Smaller**, because it is the best choice for the best display unless, if one is having some problems with the eyesight. You can also adjust the resolution, adjust the brightness, calibrate colour, change display settings, connect to a projector, adjust ClearType text, and see the custom text size, also known as (DPI) or the Dot Per Inch. Good quality pictures use hundreds of DPI on your computer or device for them to look the way they are. You can also view the personalization or devices and printers from here, using the links on the bottom on the left of the display window. You can go to other links and windows, such as devices and printers, as these are part of the Control Panel in Windows.

Figure 45: Windows Mobility Centre

Windows Mobility Centre—you can use this feature to do more with your computer, just in one place. The feature window is as shown below. You can now adjust many things such as brightness, sound, battery, network or internet and many more. You can even connect to an external display or monitor. You can synchronize, your computer with audio devices. You can use a projector for presentations. You can click the Windows Help and Support icon that looks like a question mark on any Control Panel window as shown on the far bottom-right of this window above. You can mute the sound, if you want to do so, using this feature. My battery plan is set to '**Balanced**,' but yours may differ.

In the next chapter, we are going to look at programs and features in Windows. As a system administrator, you can install and un-install programs. How do you install a program? We are going to learn how to work on this shortly. Many people think that they only need to know a little bit about computers, not much. However, if you know more about computers, you can get employed for that. You can learn a lot by yourself about computers, if you only want to do so from now onward. I encourage you to learn more, and this is the reason I wrote this book. This manual for system administrators is good for you, because it makes the advanced features simple to understand. To setup the sound on your computer does not really mean you have to take your computer to a computer wizard (expert), because you can do it, yourself, as explained in this book. Try to do it and you will see the importance of learning computing skills. You may experience sound problems, and you thought you could not fix it, yourself. I do believe that I can do anything, if I only have an interest. I self-published the same book you are reading, and many other books. I fix my computer problems, even before I could go for computer studies, and I wish you could do the same. You may do more than what I can do. I personally do not use Mobility Centre always, but it is such a great tool in Windows, because it can help you manage many settings in one place. The easiest way of getting into any Control Panel window is typing the name of the feature you want in the search box, when you clicked the Start Button. Click the **Start Button** => type **Mobility Centre** => click the **Windows Mobility Centre** icon in the search results list and the window will open. There are many ways to kill the rat (someone said), and indeed, there are many ways to run a program in Windows 7. You may be interested in "**Windows 7 For Beginners**," if you are an absolute beginner. For the brightness settings and sound settings in Windows Mobility Centre windows, you can simply press and hold the left mouse button as you drag the slider, to increase or decrease brightness or sound.

CHAPTER 4: PROGRAMS

~~**~~

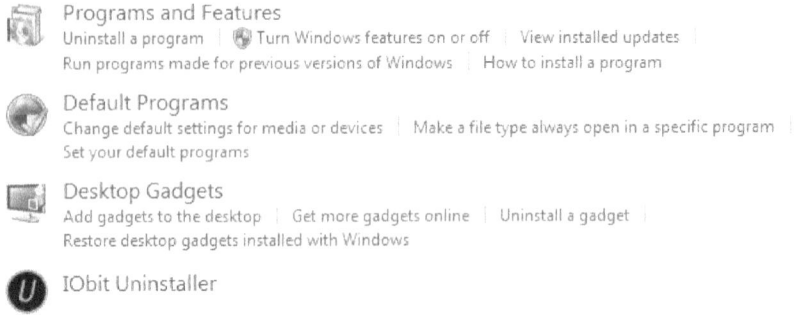

Programs and Features
Uninstall a program | Turn Windows features on or off | View installed updates | Run programs made for previous versions of Windows | How to install a program

Default Programs
Change default settings for media or devices | Make a file type always open in a specific program | Set your default programs

Desktop Gadgets
Add gadgets to the desktop | Get more gadgets online | Uninstall a gadget | Restore desktop gadgets installed with Windows

IObit Uninstaller

Figure 46: Programs

This is a place to view installed Windows applications/programs and Windows updates, installed on your computer. You can even use this feature to uninstall or remove a program.

To remind you of the Control Panel, there are eight main features, starting from **System and Security** to **Ease of Access**. The programs feature is the fourth item. We still have the **User Account Control, Appearance and Personalization, Clock, Language, and Regions**, then **Ease of Access**, to cover in this book, each as a separate chapter—chapter. If you do not see any picture clearly for whatever reasons, please try to use your computer to access the feature you want to learn. The Programs and features is the first item in the **Programs** feature. We are going to discuss this shortly. A word processing program is good for writing/typing. A program is a set of instructions, that help a computer to perform certain commands and instructions. People who make programs are computer programmers. I am one of these.

To make a program, you have to learn a programming language, a machine language. There are many programming languages on the Internet, and you can download most of them free. Microsoft uses Visual Studio, to make programs. You can download it for a fee or free. I use Visual Basic to write computer programs. You can design a window, or Graphical User Interface (GUI). GUI helps a user communicate with a machine. Every program has its unique GUI, with buttons to click to execute certain commands, based on what a programmer wants it to do. As an advanced computer user, I expect you to know all these things. You can learn more about programs from the Windows Help and Support feature, accessible from the **Start Menu** => right hand side. If you would like to be a programmer, you can learn how to do this free on the Microsoft Developer Network Web Site. Computer programming is a very good job. You can get employment anywhere in the world, if you master it.

If you do not use a program, you can remove it from your machine for performance issues. We are going to dig deep into that under programs and features in this book. You can turn off/on Windows features. You can view installed updates. You can run programs made for previous versions of Windows, learn how to install a program, uninstall a program and many more. These actions are under programs and features. You can use links to do some work with your machine. However, be careful of what you are doing. Do not remove a program, unless you are sure you do not need it.

Programs and features—here, you can uninstall a program, run programs made for previous versions of Windows, or turn Windows features on/off. You can view the installed Windows updates, and learn how to install a program.

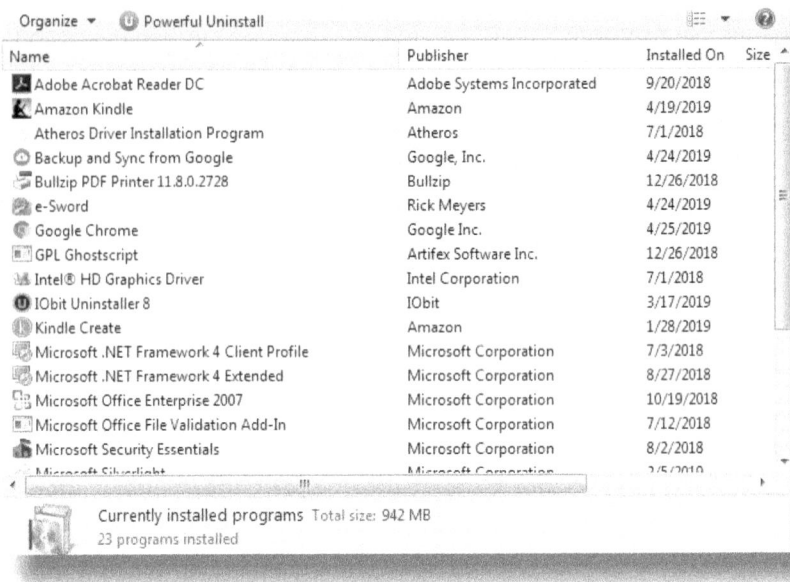

Figure 47: Installed programs

On the picture above, you can see installed programs on my computer. The programs are arranged in alphabetical order by default, but you can change the order. To change the order, click the name column, and the names will begin from Z-A. There are 23 installed programs on my computer as you can see above, and the total disk space used is 942 MB.

To uninstall a program, click on it, and then click, "**Uninstall,**" or "**Change,**" on a toolbar that will appear. You can also view installed updates or turn on/off the Windows features, using links on the far top-left corner. Someone said, "If you don't use it, then remove it." This is true with computing. You cannot allow your computer to run slowly because of programs you don't need. In this feature, you can uninstall programs you don't need. Sometimes, some applications install themselves without your knowledge. Most of these applications come with updates or because you installed a certain software. Toolbars always install programs that you may not need. These applications installed without your knowledge may slow down or even damage your computer. When you are installing new software, make sure you don't just agree with any option given. Some applications ask you to install additional software when you install them. You have to make sure you know what software you are installing. If you realized that an application (software) is causing problems to your machine, uninstall it. Many good programs can slow down your machine, and you have to ask yourself whether you really need all of them or just some. I use at least 23 programs on my machine. Most of these are updates for Windows and other software. I always make sure I check the updates before they are installed. Before learning more above software, I used to download many software, including things I do not really need. Now, I only install what I need, and leave what I do not. I once downloaded a virus with Adobe Reader updates!

The whole concept here is that when you installed many programs on your computer, it is likely that the system will slow down in the area of performance. But this also depends on your Hard Disk capacity. I wish you keep only what you can use, but as mentioned earlier, you have to be careful also as you uninstall a program. I once uninstalled my **Service Pack 1**, which my computer needed. It was a serious mistake. After removing the feature, many programs, including Skype, Office 2017, stopped working as the result. The good news is that I can download my service pack free of charge from Microsoft website! Even system administrators like me make mistakes, when it comes to uninstalling programs. The best thing to do is to check and check again the programs selected before you click the "**Uninstall**," or the "**Change**," on the toolbar.

Default programs—this is where you can set which programs you want to open certain files by default. You can now change the default program settings for media or devices, set your default programs, or make a file type always open in a specific program. You must be very careful in setting the default programs, because you may end up opening all file types, using one program, and that can cause your computer to malfunction!

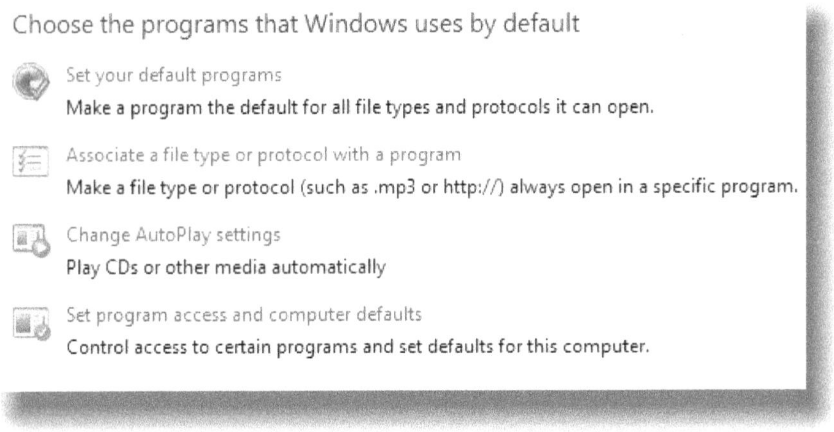

Choose the programs that Windows uses by default

Set your default programs
Make a program the default for all file types and protocols it can open.

Associate a file type or protocol with a program
Make a file type or protocol (such as .mp3 or http://) always open in a specific program.

Change AutoPlay settings
Play CDs or other media automatically

Set program access and computer defaults
Control access to certain programs and set defaults for this computer.

Figure 48: Default programs

Default programs are programs that you use always or frequently. Here, you can set your default programs, or associate a file type or protocol with a program. You can even change the **AutoPlay** settings, or set the program access and computer defaults. Use the links to these mini features under this feature to set your computer to do what you want it to do for you. Default programs are used to run files associated with them, but you have to be careful when you associate files with programs. Be very careful about the linking of programs with file types! If your desktop icons show in one program, this could be a result of linking one program to open all file types on your computer. You can use this feature to un-associate file types, and this may fix problems.

Desktop gadgets—this is part of the display feature, but it is also under the Programs' feature. You can add gadgets to the desktop, restore gadgets installed with Windows, get more gadgets online, or uninstall a gadget you don't need.

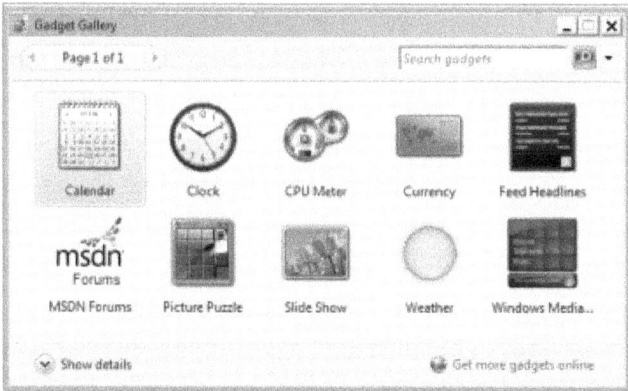

Figure 49: Gadgets window

Gadget gallery is on the **Start Menu** when you clicked 'All Programs' link. You can then look for **Desktop Gadget Gallery** and click on it. There are many different gadgets. Your gadgets may look different from mine. The MSDN for example, may not be on your computer. I am a program developer/software programmer, which is why you can see Microsoft Developer Network gadget, since I use it mostly.

To activate a gadget, click on it using the left-mouse button twice, quickly (double-clicking), and it will then show up in the right hand side of your desktop screen. You may not use all the gadgets at once. Use the ones you like, and leave the rest. You can even setup gadgets, using three buttons, depending on the gadget type. You can uninstall a gadget, if you want to, using (x) or the close button. You can drag and drop a gadget on the desktop, or you can expand it. Some gadgets cannot be expanded. Some have more functions and settings. The clock gadget for example, can be set to show a second hand, and you can even change the clock name to something like Nairobi. You can choose from many clock styles.

Open your computer gadget now, and test yourself, activating some gadgets and change their settings. Make sure you use the gadgets you trust, because any third-party software can be a virus, unless you know the company that makes it. As mentioned earlier, you have to be very careful with installing programs. Desktop gadgets can be viruses or any other malicious software, which can harm your computer and you. How can a virus harm me? If a virus can steal your bank account details, including passwords, the owner of that virus can withdraw all your money. Could that be harmful to you, personally? Be careful installing anything from the Internet, unless you know what it is. Now, you have learned about desktop gadgets. There are many different types of gadgets that you can get from the Internet on the Microsoft site. There are Administrative Accounts and Standard Accounts. Administrative Accounts have more rights and controls than Standard Accounts, and that means you must have an administrative rights in order for you to explore the Control Panel.

In Windows XP, the **C: Drive** is not even accessible, because all the folders in that directory are hidden by default for security reasons. The Guest Account is one. You can decide to turn it on/off. If you turned on a Guest Account, you have to give it a password. The reason is that anyone can log into your computer using any active account with no password. This can allow anyone to browse your folders, your important documents without your permission. Because this feature is under **System and Security** feature, you can now see the reasons why you have to create a password for each account on your computer. Always lock your computer when going away for a while—Windows Key + L.

CHAPTER 5: USER ACCOUNTS & FAMILY SAFETY

~~**~~

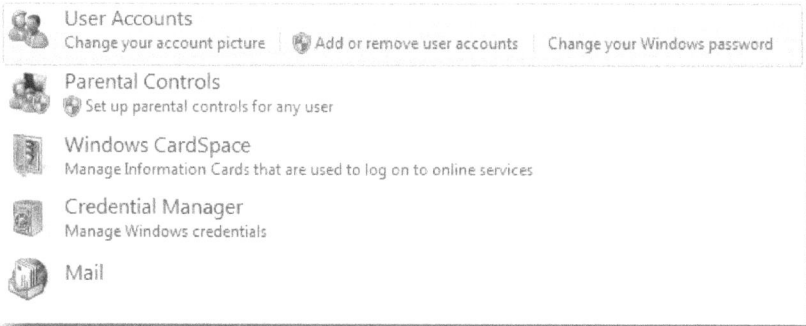

Figure 50: Accounts & Family Safety

As mentioned earlier, this is a place where you set controls on how people use your computer. You can create user accounts for yourself, or for other people who may use your computer, like other family members. You must set up passwords for each account or your computer will be at risk.

User Accounts—these are accounts for users. Only one person can use a personal computer, such as a desktop or laptop at a time. Here, you can change your account picture, add or remove accounts, change your Windows password, and many other controls. You must have administrative privileges to do all these. I can change my password or remove it completely, if I want to, by clicking the right link, and another window will open, where I can do the actions. Removing a password require me to enter the old password exactly before creating a new one. I cannot remove my password until I have to enter it first before I could remove it. I can change my picture or my account type. I can also manage another account, or change UAC settings. On the far left hand side, I can see many links that I can use, if I want to. The links here can allow me to manage my credentials, create a password reset disc, link online IDs, manage my file encryption certificates, configure advanced user profile properties, or change my environment variables—data. I can also view Parental Control, using the link on the bottom-left corner of the window.

Parental Controls—you need these controls as a parent, to manage how your children use a computer when you are away from home. You can also set Parental Controls for any standard user. The Parental Controls help you control what your children can do with a computer, especially in your absence. It is like a spying tool, watching for you what your children can do. You can set these controls on any standard accounts, not administrative accounts. It is advisable that you use a Standard Account so that you don't make serious mistakes. It is possible to make mistakes, even if you are an advanced computer user. Learn more about Parental Controls and set one up for your computer. Standard Accounts are safer, and you can still manage your system using a Standard Account with fewer mistakes.

To manage your system using a Standard Account, enter your password when the system asked. Your password must be an Administrative Account password. If you enter the Standard Account password, you will not be allowed to modify or explore features of Control Panel. You can only edit accounts when you have an Administrative Account rights. You can create, remove, rename, or manage many things in other accounts, when needed. I create accounts on my computer and I install computer programs, because I am a system administrator. This feature lists all active accounts. You have to create a password for each user for security purposes. You can create a new user account here, or learn more about the reasons to create that account. You can learn how to install additional controls using a link. The link on the far top-left is game rating systems. The link below on the bottom-left corner of the window is a User Accounts link, which will take you back to the main User Accounts window, when clicked.

Windows Card-Space—you can set and manage the information a computer uses when you log on to other services online. Here, you can manage information cards used to log into online services. The image cannot be captured when the Windows Card-Space is running. This is the reason why you cannot see the picture for this item.

Credential Manager—you can manage Windows credentials here. This is where you set up certificates and other information about you, which Windows can use when you want to sign a document and other services on your computer. This is where Windows keep credential or critical information about any user. Your passwords and usernames are managed here. You can add a Windows credential or a certificate based credential. You can also add a generic credential. My generic credential is a **SkyDrive/OneDrive**, an online backup system from Microsoft. You must know the network server address in order to add the credentials. For my SkyDrive/OneDrive network address, see below. The password characters are hidden for security reasons. I hope you like the feature. You can edit credentials, or remove them completely from your backup vault. Rolution is another third-part vault provider, online—for a fee!

Mail—this is where you can setup Windows Mail. Windows Mail has been the service, just like Windows Live ID, that you can setup. We also have Microsoft Office Outlook. When you clicked the mail icon this is what will come up. You can now set up your e-mail accounts. You can use the "**E-mail Accounts**," to setup the accounts. You can also use, "**Data Profiles**," to choose where you want the Outlook program to store the data on your computer. You can setup multiple profiles of e-mail accounts, using the button, or you can close the window. I rarely use Outlook mail, because of many reasons. This program keeps all your emails on your Internal Hard Disk. Depending on the types of messages you receive, your Hard Disk will get full. Imagine if you receive attachments every day from email contacts, these will all be stored on your hard disk. I love using web-based email services like Gmail (Google Mail) or Yahoo, and others, because they do not keep my email messages on my Hard Disk. Imagine if anyone hacked into your system, your private messages will be read! Nevertheless, you may love this email service because of its features. Outlook program looks like any other Microsoft Office program. You can manage your emails easily. You can read the downloaded messages even when you are offline, and many people like this feature. With Gmail, you cannot read any email message, if not connected to the Internet. There are many email services and for your information, I do not even know many of them. If you love Outlook, go ahead and setup the program and begin to use it at anytime from now.

Remember, you may need Internet connections to complete the setup process—first time users. More options are available on the Outlook window, if you wish to learn more about how to set it up. If you are using an organization computer, you may like using Outlook for many reasons. For quick formatting, Outlook is one of the best tools. Nowadays, even Gmail and Yahoo have all the tools for formatting your email messages. There is even an online version of Outlook on the www.outlook.com site to sign up for an account. You can use more than one account with Outlook. Outlook is the same as Windows Live ID/Microsoft Account. I have an email account with Gmail. I use it on my Microsoft account, and it works fine. I suggest you use the online version, if you can, especially if you are using your personal computer. The purpose of this suggestion is that your Hard Disk will get filled up with emails, depending on the size of your hard disk.

CHAPTER 6: APPEARANCE & PERSONALIZATION

~~**~~

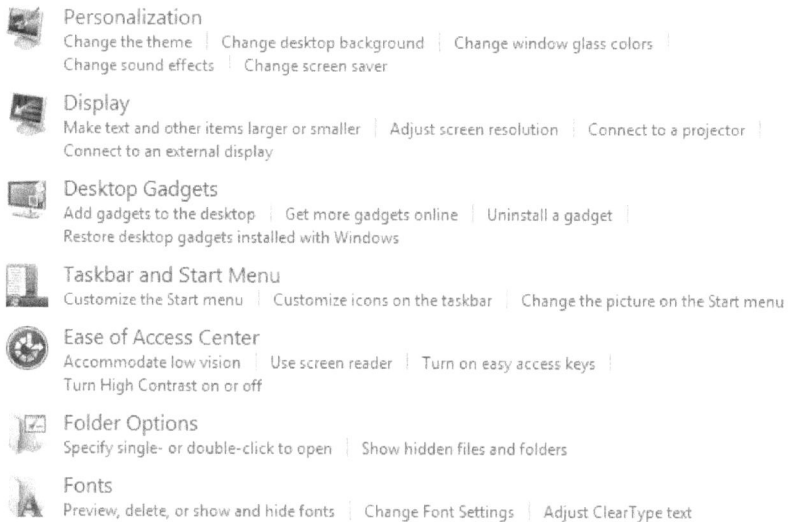

Figure 51: Appearance & Personalization

We will talk about **Taskbar and Start Menu**, fonts, display and desktop gadgets here. This is the main feature where we control how our desktop and other things on the computer appear. You may remember that some of these features have been discussed earlier, and we are aware of that (See **Part I**).

Personalization—you can change the theme of your desktop, change your desktop background, change sound effects and change the screen saver of your computer from here. This is part of the Display settings feature. You can choose a theme you want, to change your desktop wallpaper or background. You can choose the window colour, sound and screen savers here. You can change the desktop icons, mouse pointers and even your account picture from here. You can even troubleshoot problems with transparency and other aero effects. The other links to use are **Display, Taskbar and Start Menu**, and **Ease of Access**, and you can see these links on the bottom-left hand side of the window. You can also save the current new theme or get more themes online free. Be careful not to download any third-party themes because of viruses!

Taskbar and Start Menu—this is part of a desktop, and it is also part of the appearance and personalization. You can customize the Start Menu, customize icons on the taskbar, and you can change the picture on the Start Menu. This picture on the Start Menu is the current User Account picture—yours. There are three main tabs on the Taskbar and Start Menu window. You can get to this window when you right-click on the Taskbar, and then choose **Properties**, in the drop-down menu. The Taskbar tab is what we are viewing. You can lock the Taskbar, Auto-hide the Taskbar, use small icons in the Taskbar, or change the Taskbar location from bottom to top, left or right. You can customize or make changes to the notification area on the Taskbar, by clicking on "**Customize**." To learn more on this, click where it says, "How do I customize the taskbar?" You have to apply new settings before they can take effect. Click **OK** when done.

This is the Start Menu tab. Here, you can change the power button action. By default, the power button is set to **shut down**, but you can change it to something else, depending on your choice. You can change the power button action to Switch user, Log off, Lock, Restart, Sleep or Hibernate, using the drop-down menu that will appear when you click the arrow next to the shut down text.

There are two main privacy settings here, as you can see. You can select the store, display recently opened programs in the Start Menu, or store, and display recently opened items, in the Start Menu and the Taskbar or both. This helps me find the recently opened programs and items on the Start Menu when I need them.

For security seasons, lock your computer when you go away from it for a while. You can use the Taskbar and Start Menu properties window to set up the Taskbar, including the notification area icons just in one place. You have learned how to setup the Taskbar and Start Menu items. The last tab here is the Toolbar tab. On this tab, you can only add things to the taskbar, such as the address, links, Tablet PC Input Panel and the Desktop. You may need some of these things, and if that is true, select the check box next to the item you want, and it will activate. You can then click **Ok** or the **Apply** button.

Next, we are going to learn about folder options, where we can setup folder-browsing, view, and search options.

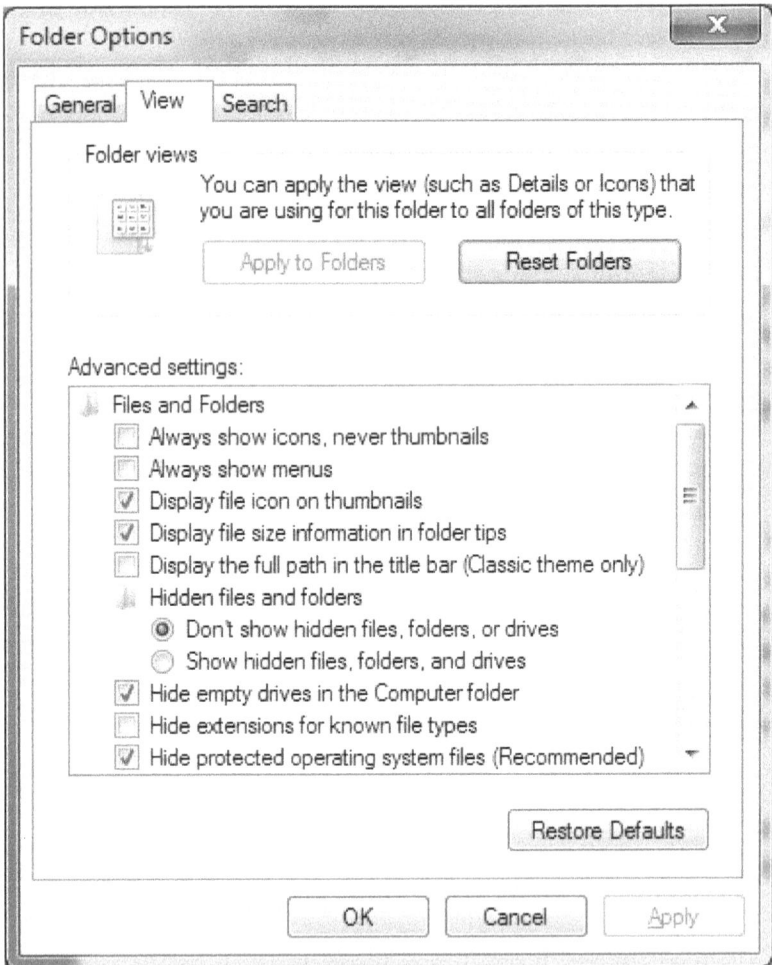

Folder Options—this is where you can set how you want the folders to appear on your computer. You can specify whether to single-click or double-click a folder to open it. Have you ever known this before? You can also show hidden files and folders from here. You can make Windows show you file extensions, if you want because sometimes you have to know file extensions to determine file types. However, to quickly open the Taskbar and Start Menu properties window, right-click the Taskbar, then choose **Properties** and you are there. On the toolbar tab, you can select the items you want to add to the Taskbar and then click the

"**Apply**" or "**Ok**" button, and your settings will be saved. The **Folder Options** feature in Windows 7 allows you to change many things about how you want your folders to look like. You can even change the filename extensions from here. There are three tabs on this folder option feature. The **general** tab above allows you to set the browsing for folders option. You can also change how the mouse works on folders such as single-click to open an item (point to select), or double-click to open an item (single-click to select). The last option is set that way by default, but now you have learned how to change it. You can also set the navigation pane. If you want your computer to show all folders in the selected folder, then select that option. If you want the folders to expand automatically into the current folder, then select this option as shown above. You can even restore defaults, or factory settings for this. Click the "How do I change folder options?" link, to open Windows Help and Support. The **view** tab helps you change many things, including the file name extensions' view. The **search** tab helps you to set search options such as what to search for, how to search and what to do when the item you are searching for is not found, using basic search.

Fonts—do you know where to find and set your fonts on your computer? Fonts are very important components of a computer, because everything you do, especially with text, appears the way it appears because of fonts. You can now preview, delete, or show and hide fonts in your system. You can also change font settings and adjust ClearType text, a feature in Windows, which helps you adjust how you want the text to appear on the screen. You can preview, delete, or show and hide the fonts installed on your computer here. Select the font and choose the action from the toolbar menu and you will be ready.

Display—as normal, you can make text and other items larger or smaller, connect to the external display, adjust the screen resolution, and connect to a projector, using this feature on Windows. We have discussed display features earlier.

Desktop—as part of the appearance and personalization, desktop is where most of the appearances take place. You can add gadgets to the desktop, restore desktop gadgets installed with Windows, get more gadgets online, or uninstall a gadget you do not want.

Ease of Access Centre

This is another feature under appearance and personalization. You can accommodate low vision, turn high contrast on/off, use screen reader, and turn on the easy access keys here. We will talk more on this in chapter eight. Jump to that chapter to see more details on the Ease of Access Centre. Now, you can change the display on your computer screen (Size) and set it to default (100%) since many screens do not support more than hundred percent display zooming. You can change your wallpaper or desktop background and you might already know how. However, if you do not know how to setup your desktop background, follow these steps and you will be done. Click the desktop using the right mouse button, choose **Personalization**, and click the **desktop background**. Select the background you need and click **save changes**, and you are done.

I love learning computing, alone. A computer is a tool that can also teach us how to use it as mentioned earlier. Use it and learn more by yourself. A teacher does not give the student hundred percent in class, because learning involves both the teacher and the student. The student seems to take the biggest portion in the learning process. The same idea applies here in learning about computers. I love learning through practice. I expect my readers to do the same. You might have selected this book because someone told you about it, or because you stumbled with it online and you wanted to see what the title seems to promise. Now, you have seen the book.

It is a practical guide where you are expected to test yourself by practicing what you have learned. To learn more about this just move to the next chapter in this book and begin your learning process.

The next item to look at is the clock, region, and language. A computer uses a digital clock on the bottom-right of the desktop screen. You can also use this clock icon to set the clock to the local time.

CHAPTER 7: CLOCK, REGION & LANGUAGE

~~**~~

Date and Time
Set the time and date | Change the time zone | Add clocks for different time zones
Add the Clock gadget to the desktop

Region and Language
Change location | Change the date, time, or number format
Change keyboards or other input methods

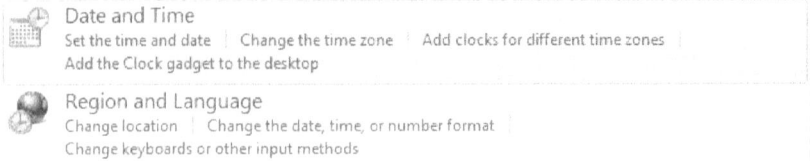

Figure 52: CLOCK, REGION & LANGUAGE

Under this feature, you can set the date and time to your local time, and you can set different time zones on your computer. You can even add the clock gadget to the desktop as discussed above.

Date and time—set the date and time, add the clock gadget to the desktop, change the time zone, and add clocks for different time zones and more. One easy way is to click the clock icon on the far bottom-right, then choose the change date, and time settings. A window will open on the far left hand side of your computer screen. To set the time, click on the clock, and then choose the *"Change date and time settings..."* and a window will open on the far left of the computer screen where you will set the time and date. There will be many options to choose from, but at least you have an idea of what to do now. The time is affected by the region or place where you live, and because of this, there are many different time zones in the world.

Region—you can now change the location, change keyboard or other input methods, change the date, time, or number format here. To change a keyboard means changing a language to another language. A language must be installed on your computer in order for you to use it. The fonts for that language must also exist on your system. For me to type the word (tiëm) I must have the fonts for that language that puts two dots on top of an (e) as you can see above. This word in my language means victory. You can find many fonts online for free and some for a fee. You can even download Keyman Desktop, a computer program that will help you type in your language. The website is www.tavultesoft.com. With Keyman Desktop, you can type in many local languages in the world. You can even type in Arabic, even if you do not have a physical Arabic keyboard. This is amazing. I use it to type in Nuer, Dinka, Hebrew, Arabic, and Greek. I can even add more languages, if I want to do so. You may already know some programs that you can use to help you type in your language just like the Keyman Desktop. You can use those programs to help you type in your language, if you know how to use them. I love Keyman Desktop. I use it for translating books from English to Dinka or Nuer languages. You may love the software, too. Do you know that if your computer's time and date do not match the international time, your computer will not update on the right time as scheduled? This is why it is important for you to use your local time settings in order for the system to work as required. The time setting does not only serve one aspect, but more than one.

CHAPTER 8: EASE OF ACCESS

~~**~~

Figure 53: EASE OF ACCESS

This feature can make someone with natural problems enjoy a computer. If you have been having seeing, hearing, or reasoning problems, use this tool to help you use your computer normally, just like any other person with no problems at all. This is the goodness of technology. I appreciate what Microsoft software developers have done in this area. You can use this feature, in case you have a natural problem. Some people could not see or hear well, so they can make use of the Ease of Access feature in Windows.

Ease of Access Centre—here, you can set up and let Windows suggest what is good for you, but you have to choose the options that suit your needs. You can even change how your mouse works or how you want it to work. You can optimize visual display, and even change how your keyboard works. You can also replace sound with visual cues, especially if you have hearing problems. You can choose to always read the section load, or scan this section by using the checkboxes next to each option. You can optimize the computer for blindness, or optimize visual display. You can set up an alternative device or you can make the mouse easier to use.

Speech Recognition—this is where you can set your computer to listen to what you say, and it can do what you tell it to do exactly as you want—commands. You can read your notes as the computer types them, but you have to pronounce words properly, or you will not see what you expected. You can simply start the Speech Recognition tool, but you must have microphones connected to the computer before you start the feature—some computers. You can set up the microphones, but it has to be connected to the computer or the program will fail to start normally—will start on some computers. Some computers do not need setting or headphones when doing Speech Recognition. The reason is they already have microphones built-in to the system. You can even train your computer to better understand you! You can then open the Speech Reference Card. You can perform all these tasks, using the right links. You can train your computer until it knows your accent, your voice. After that, you can talk to the computer and it will not have problems hearing. You can now write on the paper and then dictate your work and the computer will type for you what you say! Can you see how useful a computer is?

We have come to the end of this. Thank you so much for reading through. I hope you loved the item. You can write your book review and let me hear what you think about the book. Let me hear your suggestions and comments.

Write to me at maluthabiel@gmail.com

BOOK 3: WINDOWS OPTIMIZATION TIPS

Introduction to Windows Optimization Tips

This is about how to securely find and fix common computer errors without the ICT personnel's help. Following the steps given in this book will surely help you resolve many common computer problems. The book is all about my experience on how I fixed common computer errors for the last 4 years (2010—2013). It is my daily work. This book gives you all the steps I take.

You can use the book to fix your computer errors, or use it as your tool to help others with the same problems. You may get some money as the result of using this book correctly, because people with problems will pay you after you helped them out. It is a result of my experience with Microsoft Windows and its tools. As a business tool, I mean using it to fix computer problems, and ask for a fee. It is your tool, whether you buy it, or obtained it free from the Smashwords website. If you love the tool, please share it with others, and they will thank you for it. The book also refers you to other books with more detailed information about certain issues discussed. The main book is **Windows 7 Control Panel**. This contains details about Windows 7 and Windows 8/10. If you are using Windows XP, get **Windows XP Control Panel**.

CHAPTER 1: DISK CLEANUP TOOL

~~**~~

First, you need to know what Disk Cleanup is. Disk cleanup is a tool included in Windows Operating System. If your computer gets slow to respond, then you need this tool to fix the problem. There are many reasons for a computer to start responding slowly. One main reason is that it accumulates useless data or files you do not need. Disk Cleanup will clean those files. These are not your documents or files.

Starting Disk Cleanup Tool

How do you run or start the Disk Cleanup Tool? Click the Start Button, type **Disk**. In the results list under programs section, you will see all the results for disk. Click on the **Disk Cleanup** and the program will begin to run. The order for any tool searched will depend on your computer. The recently used tool usually shows up on top when you search for the same tools.

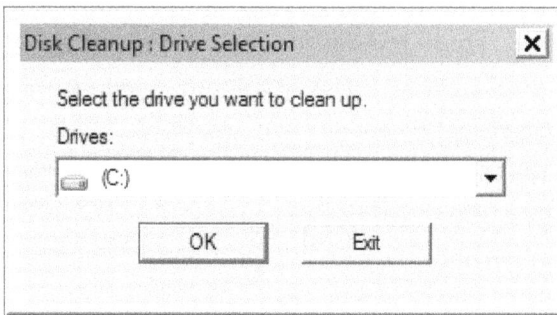

Figure 54: Disk Cleanup

As you can see, **Disk Cleanup** tool is now running. It is asking you to select a disk to clean up. When you use your computer for some time, it gets dirty just, like when you use your house. You need to sweep your house, so that it is clean and the same concept applies to a computer. Now, select the disk you want to clean. My default disk is (**C:**), but yours may differ. You can choose to Exit or click **OK** to start cleaning up the selected disk.

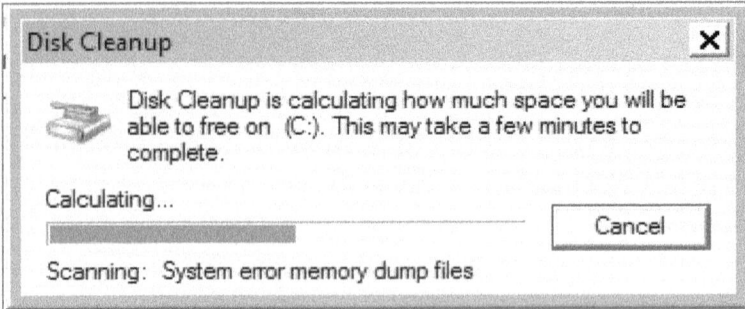

Figure 55: Calculations

After clicking **OK**, a window will appear. This window shows Disk Cleanup is calculating how much space you will be able to free on disk (**C:**). This may take a few minutes to complete as you can see above. You can see that the tool is currently scanning system error memory dump files. Can you imagine that whenever an error occurs on your system the computer captures and keeps all those useless files on your hard disk? You do not need these files. They are not important. The system always record whatever you do on your computer. These records are stored on your hard disk. Some records are good, because they are about some errors that can be sent to Microsoft. Your system may use these reports to download the right updates. However, the reality is that you do not need all these files. You have to clean them up, using Disk Cleanup tool.

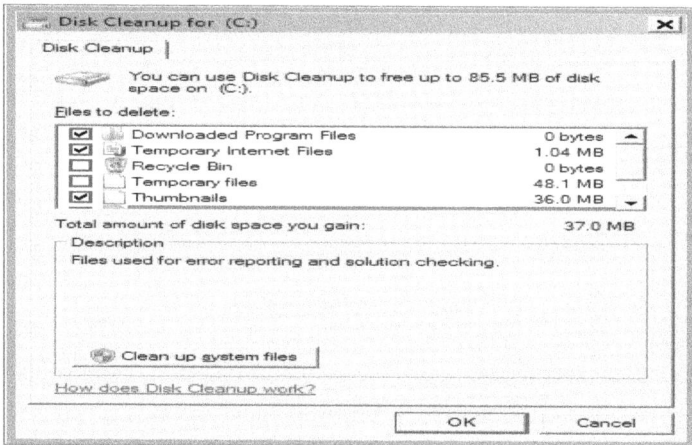

Figure 56: Selecting Files to Delete

After calculations, you still have a choice to make. The computer will ask you to choose what you want to delete. For our example above, we can clean up a disk space of 85.5 MB on our disk (**C:**). You can select a checkbox on the left side of a file title. Here, you can see "**Downloaded Program Files**" showing 0 bytes. This means there is nothing to delete here. You can see the "Temporary Internet Files, Recycle Bin, Temporary Files, and Thumbnails," all these files have different sizes. Now, select the files to delete, and click **OK**. You can also click **Cancel** to cancel the operation. Below the files to delete is a total amount of disk space you will gain and mine shows 37.0 MB. Below that is a description section of the selected files. When you select the Recycle Bin, the description section will explain to you what the Recycle Bin is and what it does. It will read, "Recycle Bin contains files you have deleted from your computer. These files are not permanently removed until you empty the Recycle Bin." If you are not sure of what you have in the Recycle Bin, you can leave it. You can click the **view files to clean**, or hit **clean up system files**. You can also use the link that reads, "*How does Disk Cleanup work?*" To learn more about this tool from the Windows Help Support feature. If you are sure you want to delete the unwanted files from your system, just click **OK** and the following window will appear—see below.

117

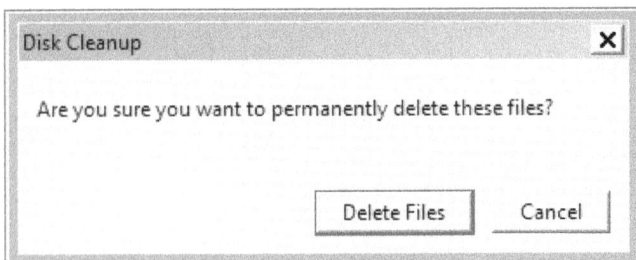

Figure 57: Confirm delete

This means Disk Cleanup Tool is asking you if you are sure to delete the selected files. Click **Cancel**, if you want to make some changes or proceed by clicking "**Delete Files**," and the tool will begin its work. If you click **Cancel**, you will have to run the tool again from the beginning. The tool is asking, "**Are you sure you want to permanently delete these files?**" This means the files will be deleted from your hard disk permanently, if you choose to do so. It is safe to delete files except if you selected the Recycle Bin, and you are not sure if you have important files in it.

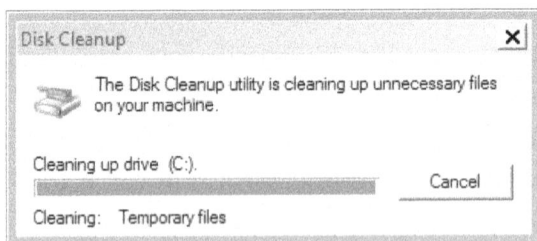

Figure 58: Deleting progress

After clicking "**Delete Files**," this window opens, and you can see that it is cleaning the files. Disk Cleanup utility is cleaning up unnecessary files on your machine to free some disk space. It also shows the drive that is being cleaned, and the files being cleaned at this particular step as you can see above. After the cleanup is done, it will just exit or close without telling you. Just as easy as that, your system will surely run faster than before, if the cause of slowness was a result of unnecessary files on your internal hard disk. Disk

118

Cleanup is a free tool that came with Windows and it works fine compared to the so-called third-party tools that are for a fee. Use your free tool, and see if it can help resolve computer issues. Please make sure there is nothing important in your Recycle Bin folder before you clean it up.

What is Disk Cleanup Tool?

This window will appear when you clicked the link that asks, "**How does Disk Cleanup work?**" This is a window for Windows Help and Support feature. You can use it to learn many things about Disk Cleanup tool. It is a full book with all details. Read and learn what this tool is and what it does. I use this tool anytime I feel like to use it, especially when my computer runs slower. It is the first tool I would like you to use for the first time when you want to fix your PC's slowness.

Next, we will go deeper: Defragmenting the disk.

CHAPTER 2: DISK DEFRAGMENT TOOL

~~**~~

Just like Disk Cleanup, Disk Defragment is to rearrange files on your hard disk. This difference between the two tools is that the first one was the first tool recommended and there is a good reason for that. Disk Defragmenter is more powerful than Disk Cleanup, because it can be scheduled to run at a time specified. This tool does not clean the unwanted files, but it arranges files on your internal or external hard disks so that there is more room.

Starting the Disk Defragment Tool

Just like Disk Cleanup, you can type "**Disk**," and it will appear in the list on the Start Menu. Click the link to run the tool. There are many buttons on this tool than the first. This means there are more functions on this. Opening this tool will differ from different platforms. I use Windows 7 and Vista when I wrote this guide.

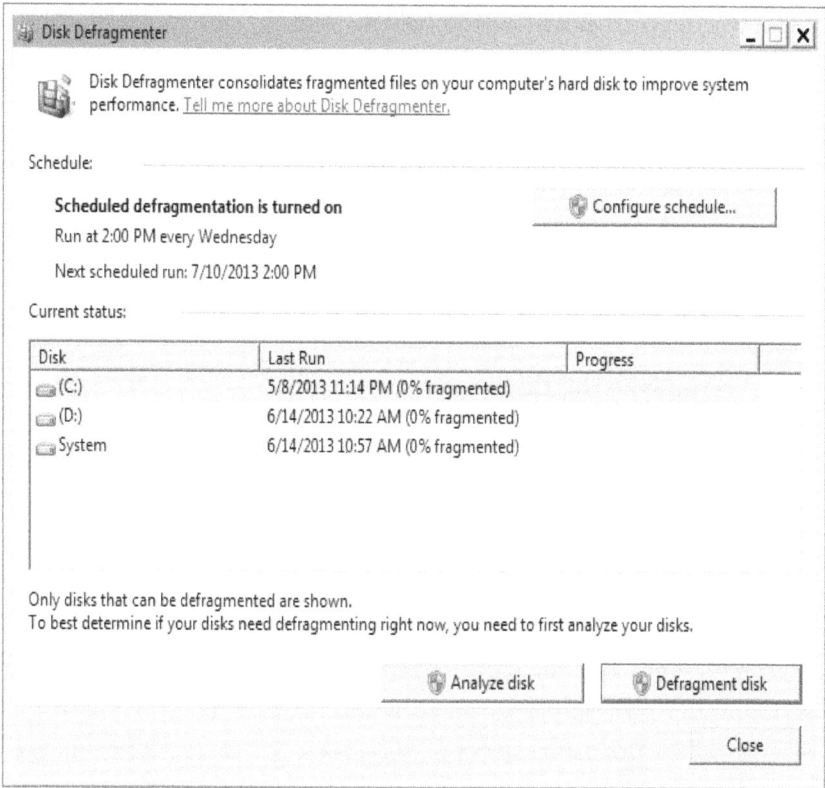

Figure 59: Disk Defragmenter

This is Disk Defragmenter. Your computer's hard disk can become fragmented during the time you use your computer. The files are somehow scattered on the disk. This tool will re-arrange the files logically so that no space is wasted. This can be the cause of the slowness of your computer, if the files are scattered on the internal hard disk. Even the external hard disks get fragmented as time goes by. You can see four buttons on the tool above. The first button is, **Configure schedule...** the other three buttons at the bottom are, **Analyse Disk, Defragment disk** and the **Close** button. My scheduled defragmentation is turn on, meaning it runs at 2:00 PM every Wednesday. The next scheduled will run on 7/10/2013 at 2:00 PM. You can click, "**Configure schedule...**" button to configure when you want the tool to run automatically. It is recommended to schedule the tool so that it does its work silently in the background without interrupting your business. All my three disks above show (0) percent fragmented, because I run the defragment tool every week. The drives are the C, D and System. The tool also shows when the disks were checked, and fragment percentage, as you can see above. First, you have to analyse the disk before you defragment it. If the level of fragmentation is about 10% or higher, you must defragment the disk as soon as possible.

How to analyze the disks

First, you have to select the disk or disks that you want to analyse, and then click "**Analyse Disk**" button. You can continue with your work as the tool analyses the disk or disks. The size of your disk and the level of fragmentation determine the time for this task to finish. As you can see, the (**C:**) drive is being analysed by the Disk Defragmenter. The analyse progress has been just 3% and it has to go up to a 100% before it can show the fragmentation level of that selected disk. I can also select all the disks, but they will be analysed one by one. The two buttons on the bottom of the window are "**Stop operation**," and the "**Close**," buttons. You can click any of them, depending on what you want to do. You can still click the "**Close**" button to close the tool. When you click "**Defragment disk**," the tool will first analyse the selected disk or disks before it can defragment them, even if you just analyse the disks. This means if the disk does not need to be defragmented the tool will not attempt to do it.

CHAPTER 3: REMOVING UNWANTED SOFTWARE

~~**~~

Removing unwanted programs is "**Uninstalling**," in the computing world. You install a program when you run its setup file or files, (executable files) with file name extension, ending with (**.exe**). However, when you are removing a program, you are uninstalling it from your computer. Many programs are installed on **C Drive** on your internal hard disk by default, including Windows.

To uninstall a program, just click on it and click the "**Uninstall**," or "**Change**," button on the toolbar that will appear on the programs and features' window. You can also view installed updates or turn on/off Windows features, using links on the far top-left corner. Someone said, "If you do not use it, then remove it." This is true with computing. You cannot allow your computer to run slowly because of programs you do not need.

In this feature of Windows, you can uninstall programs you do not need from your computer. Sometimes, some applications install themselves without your knowledge. Most of these applications come with updates or because you installed a certain software. Toolbars you may not need, always install other programs. These applications installed without your knowledge may slow down or even damage your computer. When you are installing new software, make sure you do not just agree with any option given. Some applications ask you to install additional software when you install them, and you have to make sure you know what software you are installing. If you realized that an application (software) is causing problems to your machine, just uninstall it. Many good programs can slow down your machine, and you have to ask yourself whether you really need all of them or just some. I use at least 23 programs on my machine, and most of these are updates for Windows and other software. I always make sure I check the updates before they are installed. Before learning more above software, I used to download many software, including things I do not really need. Now, I only install what I need, and leave what I do not. I once downloaded a virus with Adobe Reader updates!

The whole concept is that when you installed many programs on your computer, it is likely that the system will slow down in the area of performance. However, this also depends on your hard disk capacity. I wish you keep only what you can use, but as mentioned earlier, you have to be careful also as you uninstall a program. I once uninstalled my **Service Pack 1**, which my computer needed. It was a serious mistake. After removing the feature, many programs, including Skype, Office 2017, and more, stopped working as a result. The good news is that I can download my service pack free of charge from Microsoft website! Even system administrators like me make mistakes when it comes to uninstalling programs. The best thing to do is to check and check again the programs selected before you click **uninstall** or the **change** button on the toolbar.

How to uninstall a program

Click **Start Button** click **Control Panel** link in the Start Menu, and the window will open with many things in it. Locate **Uninstall a program** link, and click it, and another window will open with programs installed on your system listed. You can even search for the programs and features, using the search box on the Control Panel window. On the left, you can see the four main categories known as "**System and Security**, **Network and Internet**, **Hardware and Sound,** and then finally, **Programs**. Now, you can click "**Uninstall a program link**" to open programs and features. This will show you installed programs on your system. We are in the category view of the Control Panel window now, but you can change the view to any view you want (See below).

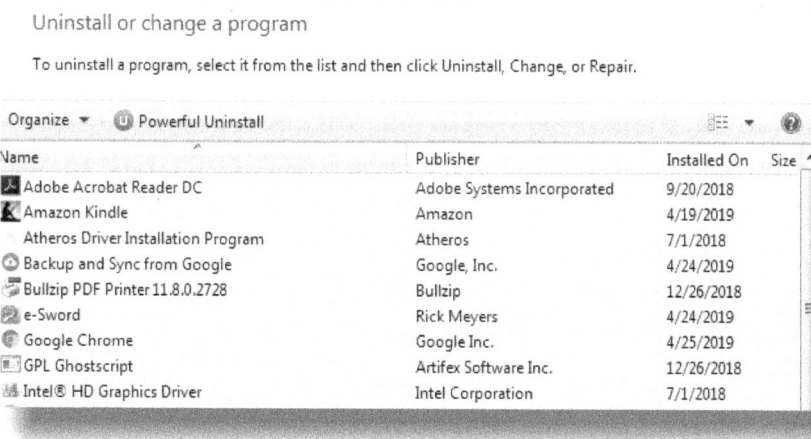

Uninstall or change a program

To uninstall a program, select it from the list and then click Uninstall, Change, or Repair.

Organize ▼   🔘 Powerful Uninstall   ▦▦ ▼   ❓

Name	Publisher	Installed On	Size ▲
🅰 Adobe Acrobat Reader DC	Adobe Systems Incorporated	9/20/2018	
🇰 Amazon Kindle	Amazon	4/19/2019	
Atheros Driver Installation Program	Atheros	7/1/2018	
☁ Backup and Sync from Google	Google, Inc.	4/24/2019	
🖨 Bullzip PDF Printer 11.8.0.2728	Bullzip	12/26/2018	
📖 e-Sword	Rick Meyers	4/24/2019	
🌐 Google Chrome	Google Inc.	4/25/2019	
▣ GPL Ghostscript	Artifex Software Inc.	12/26/2018	
🎮 Intel® HD Graphics Driver	Intel Corporation	7/1/2018	

Figure 60: Programs list

After clicking **Uninstall a program**, a window will appear, and this is the window for programs and features (above). Here, you can select a program to remove, and then click **Uninstall** in the toolbar. You can also doubt click a program to do the same thing. Windows Installer will take you through the uninstalling process. Make sure you know the program you want to remove before you remove it. Some programs are part of your system, and removing them will alter the functions of your computer, or the whole machine will stop working. I once removed a program called Microsoft NET Framework 4.0, thinking it has been an update, and this made many programs to stop working. However, if you are sure you do not use a program remove it as soon as possible. Removing unwanted programs is the best way to restore your computer's speed. When you use a computer for the very first time after purchase, it runs very fast, and the reason is there were few programs installed. However, as you begin using it for a while, it also responds slower as time goes by. Microsoft suggests if you do not use a program remove it from your system. Some programs will ask you to either remove them or repair them, and you have to choose one thing. There are slight differences on how to remove

125

programs, depending on a program. I have 23 programs installed, and most of these are program updates (0) bytes. You can also use step 6 to uninstall programs from your computer. This means you can use a third-party tool to uninstall a program. IObit has a tool called IObit Uninstaller, and I use it most of the time to remove *stubborn* programs from my computer. The reason for using this tool is that it safely removes unwanted program without leaving any segments in the registry. Windows Installer/Uninstaller does not remove everything from registry.

Next, let us look at system restore tool.

CHAPTER 4: SYSTEM RESTORE TOOL

~~**~~

System Restore tool is used when your computer could not start as normal. The disadvantage of this tool is that when you take long after you have a problem, the restore points may get deleted, and this means you cannot use them anymore. System restore points are created based on your computer settings. If a restore point is **off**, then you have to turn it **on**, so that when there is any critical issue, such as Windows Update, or any other important event, the system will create a restore point, as soon as possible, could problems occur. You can create this under system protection in the Windows Control Panel.

To create a system restore point, click **Start Button** and type **"System Restore"** and a link to the tool will appear. Click on the link and a window will appear where you will have to set a restore point. Click on the disk you want to create the restore point on. Click the **Configure** and choose what to restore. Click **Apply**. The system protection will be turned on for that disk. You can restore system settings and previous versions of files, only restore previous versions of files, or turn off system protection (Not recommended for **C Drive**).

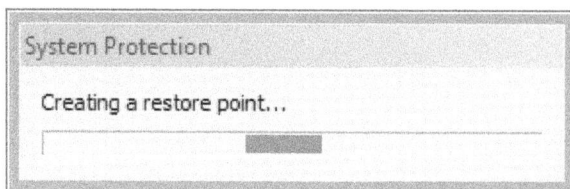

Figure 61: Creating a Restore Point

You can create a system restore point before you install or remove software, if you think it may cause a serious error to your computer. Nevertheless, you have to enable a system restore as explained above. Other third-party tools help you create system restore points whenever you remove a program on your computer. Installing a new program may change your computer settings, depending on the program. That is why you need to create a system restore point before you remove or install a program. Removing or adding a program to your computer can affect your machine in different ways based on the program you are installing or removing.

If you are using a Standard Account, the computer will ask you to enter an administrator password before you open or access the System Restore tool. System Restore tool does not work on all computers and this is not recommended. You can turn on the system protection for your **C: Drive**, in order to save the system restore points when you need them. You need restore points every day, but they must be deleted automatically or else they will also fill your internal hard disk and temper with your system performance.

There are many options to choose from when it comes to system restore functions, and you can learn most of these options practically. It is your assignment to use most tools in this book. Learning through practice is the best way to learn.

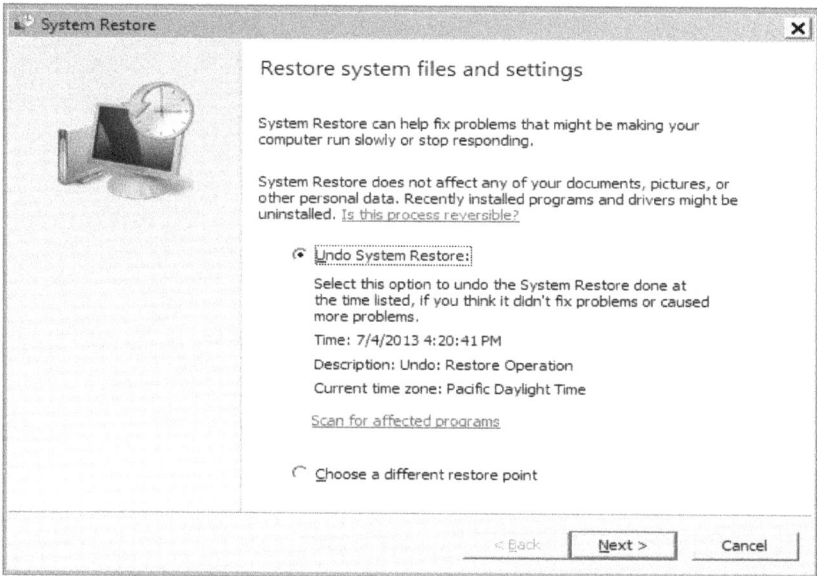

Figure 62: System Restore

Because I have done a system restore before I wrote this, the first option above is to **Undo System Restore**. However, yours may show something else. I can run a system restore from here, or I can choose a different restore point. System restore may not work if there are no restore points created before the problem occurred on your system. After you have selected the restore point by date and time, click **Next**, to continue. After choosing the restore point, you can click **Finish**, and this is to confirm your restore point. After you have confirmed the restore point, you will see a warning message saying, *system restore could not be interrupted after it starts.* Just continue and the computer alone will do the rest of the steps. The computer will restart after the restoration process, and it will report whether the restoration was successful or not.

If the restoration failed, you have to start again and choose a different restore point, until you succeed. Please, note that if anything prevents your computer from starting as normal, consider System Restore tool. It is the best secure tool I love to use most of the time. I recommend it. I love the tool because it can resolve

129

many problems. Even if a virus infected your system, and you run this tool, the virus may permanently be removed together with the newly installed programs. This is because this tool removes the newly installed programs, but it will not remove your newly created documents.

CHAPTER 5: SYSTEM REPAIR DISC

~~**~~

System Repair Disc is a disc that you can create for the future use, in case your computer refuses to work. You can use the disc to restore or repair the computer. It may take about 4 to 5 DVDs, depending on the size of your system files. This is a complete backup of the system, including your installed programs. Windows reminds you to create some backups for your files and system, but a System Repair Disc is not for your documents. It is for your system and programs only.

Starting the System Repair Disc Creator

Click **Start Button** and then type, **System Repair Disc**. A link will appear. The link will read, **"Create a System Repair Disc,"** click on the link to run the tool. After running the tool, it will ask you to select an external drive or disc where you will save the disc details and files. The drive must be a CD or DVD. It is recommended to use DVDs, not CDs because it will save you time. System Repair Disc Creator is part of the administrative tools. This means you must have the administrator privileges to use it. You will be asked to either confirm your rights, or provide a password and the username to use the tool. Confirm the required information and proceed.

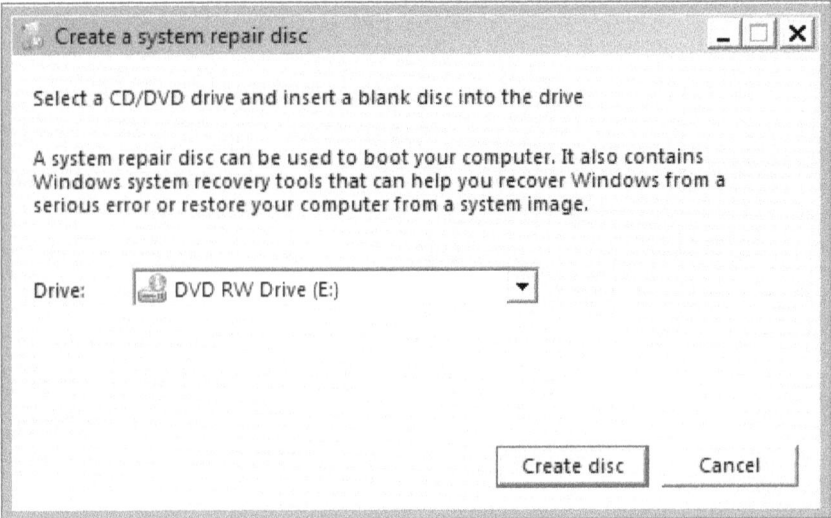

Figure 63: System Repair Disc

Now, you can select a drive, and click **Create disc** as shown above. You can also cancel the operation in case you have changed your mind. A system repair disc can be used to boot (Start) your computer. It also contains Windows system recovery tools, which can help recover Windows from a serious error, or to restore a computer from a system image. Can you see how important this disc is? You must insert a disc (DVD RW Drive) before you click **Create disc**, as shown above. The disc must be writable or else it will not work. You can also use a third-party tool to defragment your disks. You can do many things with your third-party software, and we are going to see more about this just below.

CHAPTER 6: THIRD-PARTY TOOLS

~~**~~

Third-party tools I recommend are IObit tools. The Advanced SystemCare in all its versions is the best tool I have been using. You can use a free version, or a paid one, and you will never regret. The tools are now both system cleaners and antiviral programs. There are many versions of the Advanced SystemCare, and you can try the tool free before you pay for it. The main site to get the tool is www.iobit.com. You will enjoy the tools. There are many disk cleaners, registry cleaners and more on the Internet, and you can even try some free before you buy them. I simply recommend IObit tools, because I have been using them. I have been advertising these tools on my Facebook page and on Twitter. You may win a product code, if you talk about the product online. It happened to me with Advanced SystemCare in 2011. You have to purchase a tool after the trial period expired. You also need to know how to use those tools. Follow the instruction about how to use the tools. With this free tool, you can clean up hard disks. You can also remove malware, sweep privacy online, and fix many errors. There are over 20 tools in a toolbox, and you can use almost all of these tools freely. If you decide to purchase the paid version, then you will enjoy the tools such as Registry Fixer, Internet Booster and more. You can use many free tools from IObit such as Malware Fighter, a powerful tool to find and remove deep malware infection on your machine. You can even use Disk Defragmenter from IObit.

CHAPTER 7: ACTIVE ANTIVIRUS

~~**~~

Your antivirus program must be up to date, no matter what antivirus you have. I have realized that many people don't care whether their antivirus programs work or not. When you ask them to check what antivirus program they have, the answer will always be, "I do not know, because I am not computer wizard." If you cannot check your antivirus program, then look for someone to check it for you.

Virus Protection—this is where you view the information about your antivirus software. If there is no antivirus software installed on your computer, you will find a message here, asking you to find one on the Microsoft website. If the antivirus software is just out of date, or if turned off, you will also get a message as well, and you have to find a way to fix that problem as soon as you can.

Spyware and unwanted software protection—this is another security feature in Windows, and the antivirus software may take care of this issue as well. The Microsoft Security Essentials is capable of dealing with spyware, because it is both an antivirus software and anti-spyware. Most antivirus software came with the feature, which means you will see your antivirus listed here as well. See step 10 for more information about **Action Centre**. However, I suggest you check your antivirus. If you don't know how, you better learn how to do it. It is very important. You may not have people around you all the time to check for you the antivirus program.

To check the status of your antivirus, just look at the notification area of your computer. The notification area is located on the bottom-right corner of the computer screen, right on the Taskbar. Please check Windows 7 Control Panel for more details. Different antivirus programs have different ways to update based on the design. You will have to learn more about the program itself, if you want to keep it up to date. The Graphical User Interface (GUI) differs from program to program. Even if you do not know anything about your antivirus program, try to learn how to check it. If you do not know the antivirus program, search for **Action Centre**, and it will show you installed antivirus programs. Learn how to use **Action Centre** in **Chapter 10**.

CHAPTER 8: SYSTEM CONFIGURATION TOOL

~~**~~

System Configuration is the tool you need. It can help you resolve some computer issues. You can stop Start-up items from here, if you think these items are the cause of the problems. If many programs run at the start of your machine, these programs can slow down the computer's performance. The tool has five different tabs that you can use.

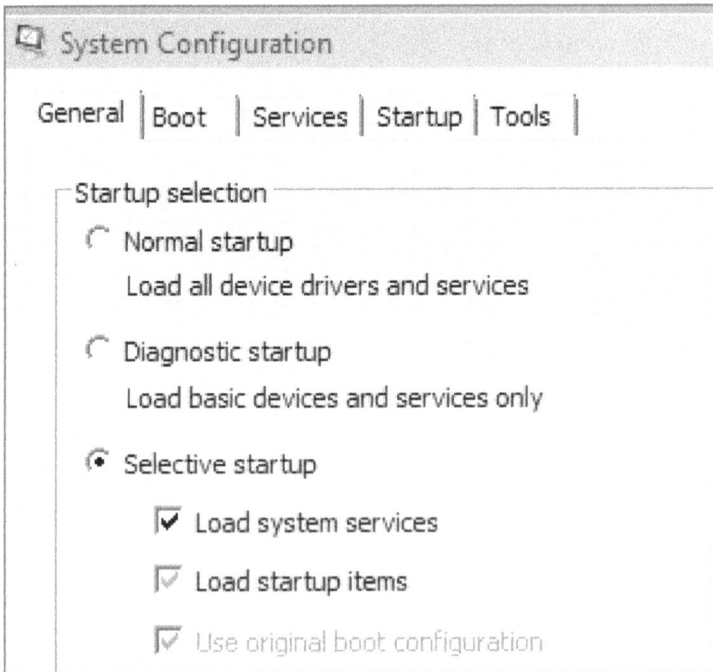

Figure 64: System Configurations

General—above is the main window of the System Configuration tool. The first tab is **General**. It is all about *"Start-up Selection."* You can choose from normal start-up, diagnostic start-up and selective start-up. You can see that I am using the selective start-up option because this can only load system services, start-up items and it can use original boot configuration. The normal start-up option loads all device drivers and services, and the diagnostic start-up can load basic devices and services only. There are other tabs such as, boot, services, start-up, and tools. We are going to discuss these tabs soon. Please, be careful with "**Boot**," tab because any change you make here will tamper with how your computer starts. You may provide your password and administrative details in order to access this System Configuration tool.

Boot—the boot time out must remain 30 seconds, or your system will not start normally. You can choose from safe boot, no GUI, boot log, base video, OS boot information, and whenever you choose one option the "set as default" and the "delete" buttons will be active. This means you can save the current settings as default or delete the setting. When you selected the "Safe boot," the other options under it will become active.

Services—you can see the running services, the manufacture names, and their status. Services column shows the names of your current services. The manufacture column shows the manufacturers of the programs, and the status shows if the services are running or not. See the picture below.

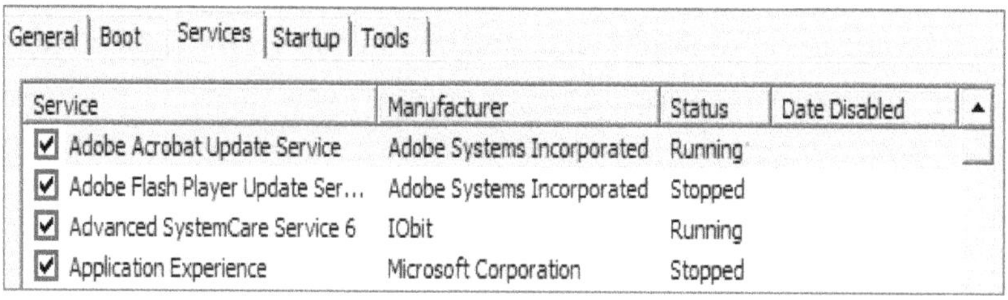

General	Boot	Services	Startup	Tools			
Service			Manufacturer		Status	Date Disabled	▲
☑ Adobe Acrobat Update Service			Adobe Systems Incorporated		Running		
☑ Adobe Flash Player Update Ser...			Adobe Systems Incorporated		Stopped		
☑ Advanced SystemCare Service 6			IObit		Running		
☑ Application Experience			Microsoft Corporation		Stopped		

Figure 65: Services

If a program or service is disabled, the "**Date Disabled**," tab will show up. You can see my services here. I have two running services and two stopped services. If you are sure you do not need a program or service, then you can stop it by making it disable. To disable a program depends on your system. My computer adds a checkbox next to the service, and un-checking the box disables the program or service. Some services may stop running alone, even if you did not disable them. However, if a service stopped running alone, it does not mean it will not run at any time. You have to disable services for better performance. You must be sure of the service you are trying to disable!

Start-up—this tab shows the list of all programs that run when you start Windows. If you know that some of these programs are not necessary, you can disable them one by one. You can even choose to disable all programs, but this is not recommended. You can use the "**Enable all**," or "**Disable all**," buttons to disable or enable the startup items. After changing the start-up options, you can then apply and click the **Ok** button to save changes. The computer will ask you to restart after clicking the **Ok** button. You can cancel the operations or click the **Help**, which will take you to Windows Help and Support feature.

Tools—the tools tab will show many tools that you can use to restore your computer. These tools include System Configuration tool. You can use tools such as, About Windows, Change UAC Settings, Action Centre, Troubleshooting and more. Each tool has its description on the right side, and you can learn more from there about the tool you want to use. You can even uninstall programs from here.

CHAPTER 9: TROUBLESHOOTERS

~~**~~

There are many troubleshooting tools in Windows. You only need to know them and learn about how they work. You can troubleshoot your computer's performance. You can troubleshoot the network issues, security issues and more. There are five main areas that you can find and fix problems with using the trouble-shooter. You do not need to have a degree in computing to know how to troubleshoot a computer problem. You only need to know what to do and how to do it. This is the main reason for my writings. I am here to teach you what I have learned personally. If you do not love doing things by yourself, you may not like this book.

To access the main troubleshooting window, click Start Button, type "**Troubleshooting**," and click on the troubleshooting link that will appear, and a window will appear. There are many tools to use under each category. You can troubleshoot Programs, Hardware and Sound, Network and Internet, Appearance and Personalization and finally, System and Security. Under each category, you will find different tools to check and find some problems to fix on your computer. This means Windows downloads other tools from the Internet during troubleshooting. Under programs, you can run programs made for previous versions of Windows. This means if a program works well on your computer before you upgraded to Windows 8, you can use this feature to make it run as it used to run.

You can run a program on Windows 7 as if it was running on Windows XP, if you use this feature. Under **Hardware and Sound**, you can configure a device, use a printer troubleshoot audio recording, or troubleshoot audio playback. Under **Network and Internet**, you can connect to the Internet, using the trouble-shooter, or access shared files and folders on other computers. Under **Appearance and Personalization**, you can display the aero desktop effects and more. Under **System and Security**, you can fix problems with Windows Update, run maintenance tasks, improve power usage, and check for maintenance issues. Most of these tasks are part of the Control Panel. You may be asked to provide an administrator password and username or just a confirmation before you can use all the tools discussed. When a problem is found and fixed, you will see a window like this below. Whether the problem was fixed or not, the computer will give you a report after trying to fix the problem. You may be asked to choose what the trouble-shooter will do with the problem. See the report below.

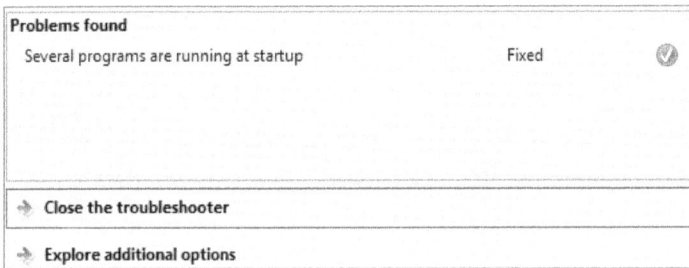

Problems found		
Several programs are running at startup	Fixed	✓

→ Close the troubleshooter
→ Explore additional options

Figure 66: Scanning Results

There were several programs running at the start-up, and some of these were stopped from running. You can choose what you want to do when troubleshooting. You can see the trouble-shooter indicates "**Fixed**," with a tick (✓) on the far right of the window. You may find out that some trouble-shooters are found under different categories such as Internet and Audio. Now, I can choose to close the trouble-shooter, or explore additional options. The right option is to close the tool, since my problem was solved.

CHAPTER 10: ACTION CENTRE

~~**~~

Action Centre is part of Control Panel in Windows. It is part of the System and Security discussed in more details in Windows 7 Control Panel (**Part IV**). You can use Action Centre to find and fix security and maintenance issues on your computer. If you cannot see the little flag in your computer's notification area, then you can run the tool as you do other tools discussed. On the bottom-left corner of the Action Centre window, you can also see the links such as Backup and Restore, Windows Update and Windows Program Compatibility Trouble-shooter. You can click these links for more actions needed. If there are, no problems, the Action Centre will look like the one below.

The Action Centre is very important, because it is where the computer tells you what to do regarding the security and maintenance of your computer. As you can see, you can fix most problems yourself here. You don't really have to have a degree in computer in order to do this. You don't have to be a mathematician to know what 5 x 10 is, and this is the same with fixing your computer issues and common problems. All you need is a manual like this, and you can practice what you learned.

To access the Action Centre, simply click **Start Button** and type "**Action Centre**," and the link will appear. Click the link to the Action Centre to see it run. There are so many things to do with Action Centre, which we will not discuss here. You can practice the features, and do more with it. You can change many settings here, if you wish. Please, see more on **Windows 7 Control Panel**, which is the same with **Windows 8 Control Panel**. The Action Centre is **Windows Security** in Windows XP. However, on Windows Vista, 7, 8, and 10, it is Action Centre. You can use many tools for your security and maintenance in the Action Centre that I will not be able to discuss in this book. You can learn all these tools practically. Someone said, "There are many ways to kill the rat," and this is true in computing as well. You can perform the same operations I am talking about in different ways. You may find another book, instructing you to do the same things, but in a different way. Keep learning and you will love reading computer books.

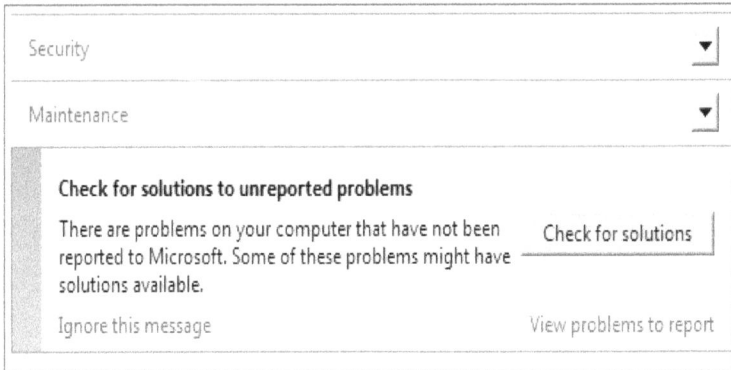

Figure 67: Security and Maintenance

I have no problem with security, but there is one issue under maintenance as you can see above. I can check for solutions to unreported problems. I can ignore the suggestion or view problems to report to Microsoft online. You can see other two links to all trouble-shooters and recovery in the picture above. You can expand the security section by clicking on the arrow pointing downwards. You can also expand the maintenance section the same way in order for you to see more details. The recovery link makes you access the recovery tools on your computer. You can restore your computer to an earlier time. I discussed this earlier.

Conclusion to Windows Optimization Tips

You have come to the end of this book. If you put into practice these simple steps, your computer will run smoothly as if you just bought it. You can do these first basic maintenance steps, yourself. These steps discussed in this book are safe and easy to use. Make your computer run as if it is brand new, by following the professional advice in this book, and you will surely enjoy the computing work. This tool was intended for computer users, who are facing computer issues. Many people want to use their money for computer maintenance, which they can do by themselves, if they only have the knowhow. You might have found this tool great, and if this is true, please give the tool to your friends, and share your knowledge. It is up to you to use the tool at home or at your business place. You can use the tool to fix many computer errors. As the writer, I know for sure that the book will pay you back, if you use it rightly.

☐

BOOK 4: MICROSOFT PAINT 2007

Running Microsoft Paint

You can start Paint like any other program. Click the **Start button**, and then look at your left hand side for Paint icon. If you cannot see it there, click **All Programs**. Click the accessories folder and then left-click on Paint. You can also type **Paint** in the search box and then left-click on the Paint icon. Remember, these steps are taken using Windows 7. A different OS may differ greatly. If you are using Windows 8/10, press Windows key + D to switch to a desktop view, to see the **Start Button**. You may need to upgrade to Windows 8.1 or Windows 10 to get back the **Start Button**.

Editing photos

You may already have an image that you want to edit with Paint, or you may create one from scratch. Whatever situation you are in, I hope these steps will help you. To edit an image that is already on your computer, you have to use the copy and paste commands on the ribbon. You can paste from file, meaning you will have to locate the image and then open it in Paint. You may also right-click the image and choose Paint as a program to open it. This is the longest step, and we will discuss it in details below.

Main Features

Now, when you have successfully opened your image in Paint, you will have to edit it or paint it. There are many tools to use here. Nevertheless, before using any painting tool, you have to know where to find them. Now, let us explore the main features.

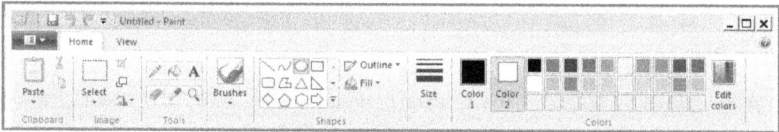

Figure 68: Paint Ribbon

Tabs—these are links in the menu bar of any program window. Tabs have tab groups under them. Most Office programs have tabs. The tools for each tab group are displayed in the "**Ribbon**," and we will discuss more about ribbon below. There are two main tabs in Paint: **home** and **view** tab. There are different tab groups under each tab for different commands and functions. You have to know these features before using Paint. However, as you practice, you will learn even more, alone.

CHAPTER 1: MICROSOFT PAINT HOME TAB

~~**~~

The Home Tab is where you find the tab groups with different commands under them. We have **clipboard**, **image**, **tools**, **shapes** and **colours** tab groups under home tab. Bear in mind that these features may change, depending on what view you are using. When you select an image, or any item, the tab for that item will be added to the main window. For example, when you are working on textboxes, a tab called "**Text**," will be added to the far right of the menu bar.

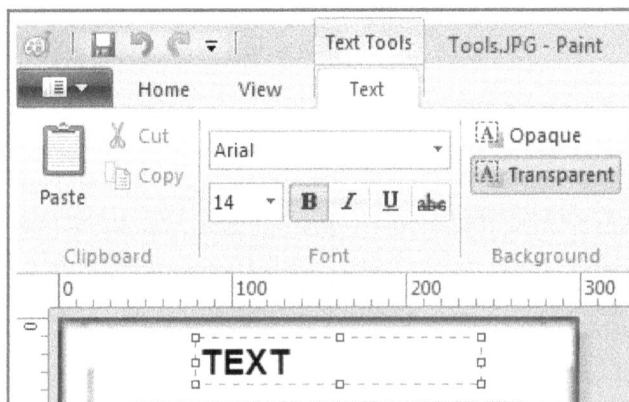

Figure 69: Inserting Text

Text Tab—this is the tab, added when working on text as shown above. Because I entered a text box in the picture above, the text tab was automatically added to the far right hand side of the main window. The **Menu Bar** contains **Home**, **View,** and **Text** tabs, because it is a place for the menu/list.

146

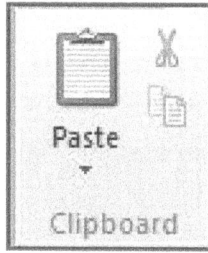

Clipboard Group—under clipboard group, there are cut and copy commands, which you can use to cut or copy text or any selected item. On the left hand side of the clipboard tab group is the "**Paste**," command, which you can use to paste copied or cut items into the current image that you are designing. Clicking on the little arrow under paste gives you two options: paste, and paste from. The paste from link/command makes you paste from a file or drive on your computer. Paste from will open the open file dialogue window when clicked, and you have to locate the picture you want to paste, and then paste it into the current image. Clicking on the upper part of the paste button above will paste whatever is in the clipboard into the image.

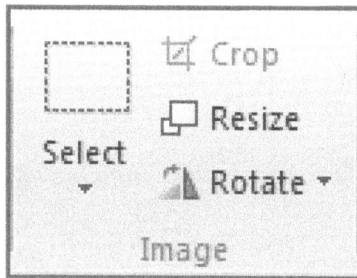

Figure 71: Image group

Image Group—under image group, you can see commands such as **crop, resize, rotate**, and **select**. Use the select command to select the area in the image, where you want to apply certain colours (more later) on this. Use the rotate command to rotate the

147

current image 90 degrees left, 90 degrees right, 180 degrees, or flip vertical and/or flip horizontal. The resize button allows you to resize pixels or percentage of the current image. You can even skew the image, if needed. To display the name for each button, resize the whole Paint window.

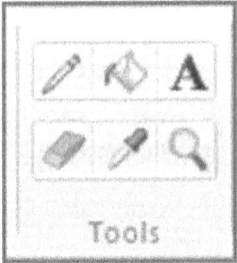

Figure 72: Drawing tools

Tools Group—under tools tab group, you have pencil, colour picker, and fill with colour tool, eraser, text, and magnifier tools/commands. These tools are useful when drawing an eye-catching book cover.

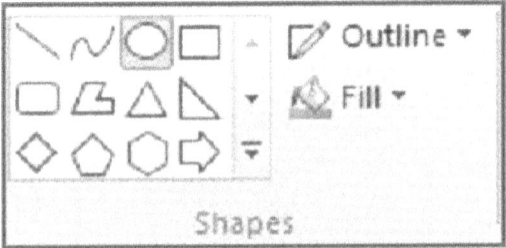

Figure 73: Shapes Group

Shapes Group—here, you have many types of shapes that you can use for your cover. You may not need all of them all the time, depending on what image you are currently working on. You can also use the fill and outline formats, when an image is selected. These commands will appear inactive if nothing selected. Use the middle arrow to see more hidden shapes. You can also use the

148

lower diagonal arrow to see all shapes at once, and choose shapes to use from there.

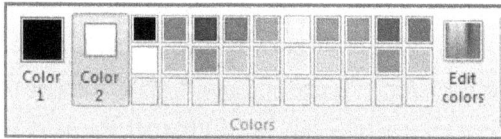

Figure 74: Paint Colours

Colours Group—under colour tab group, you can see many colours added to the ribbon, but you can still edit colours or add new colours to the ribbon for quick access. Between colours and shapes, you can also choose the size of the selector/pen. Use the **Edit colours** command to open a dialogue box, and then select the colours you want to add to the ribbon, and click **OK** to add them. You must also take note of colour 1 and colour 2 buttons. Colour 1 is for text, and colour 2 is for the background colour.

The rulers on top and left sides of Paint window are for measuring your image. When you resize images, their size also gets changed even when you are only resizing the pixels! Do not worry, simply save your image and close Paint after you are done.

CHAPTER 2: MICROSOFT PAINT VIEW TAB

~~**~~

Under the view tab, there is **zoom, show/hide,** and then **display** tab groups. Under each tab group, you find different tools. You can see that the most important tab in Microsoft Paint is the **Home** tab where you have all the functions you need for your design work. However, you also need other tabs and their tab groups.

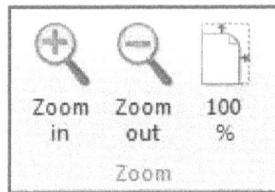

Figure 75: Zoom tools

Zoom Group—here is a place where you can zoom the image out or zoom it in. You can even use the 100% button in the zoom tab group, to zoom the current image to hundred percent. I personally use the 100% button most of the time, and I have reasons why I use it. It's selected automatically until you decide to change it.

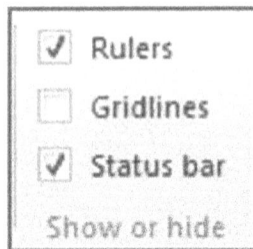

Figure 76: Show/Hide tools

Show/hide—this is where you decide to show things or hide them in the main work area of your Microsoft Paint program window. You can hide or show, rulers, status bar, or gridlines, using this tab group in Paint. It is good to show rulers, because they help you see the measurement of your picture and its size.

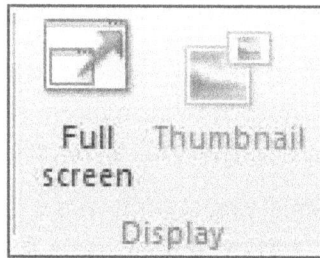

Display—this is the least important tab group in Paint, at least for me. I rarely use it. It is a place to switch to the full screen view, or use thumbnails when working with Paint. I like working in thumbnails instead of full screen. Nevertheless, you may like the opposite. In Windows 7, there are only two buttons in this tab group. Those buttons are two different commands.

Figure 78: Title bar

Title Bar—this is the area on the very top of any open window. Paint has its title bar, and when you did not save your image yet, the title bar name for the current work will be, "**Untitled - Paint.**" The name untitled is replaced by the name of your image, just after you have saved your image with a given name. On the far right of the title bar, you can see the quick access toolbar, where you can add more tools for quick access. You can find the **undo** 🔄 and **redo** 🔄 buttons on this bar as shown above. The Paint icon on the far top-left corner is for other commands you can use: **restore, move, size, minimize, maximize,** and **close** (Alt+F4).

151

Figure 79: Quick Access Toolbar

Quick Access Toolbar—when you right-click the Quick Access Toolbar you can minimize ribbon, remove items from the Quick Access Toolbar or show the Quick Access Toolbar below the ribbon. Clicking the small arrow on the Quick Access Toolbar will also allow you to add or remove items from the Quick Access Toolbar.

Save Button— like any other Quick Access Toolbar buttons, this button can be added, or removed from the Quick Access Toolbar. Use this to save your current work instead of using the Paint button discussed below. The icon for the save button resembles a floppy disk.

Paint Button—is a button on the far left corner. Like Office Button in Office programs, you can use this button to open new Paint window, save, save as, print, and do anything with the current image that you are working with.

Figure 80: Zoom slider

Zoom Slider—this is the area on the far bottom right of the open Paint window. You can use it to zoom the currently selected item or image on your work area. Like in Microsoft Office word program, the zoom slider for Paint has a plus (+) and minus (-) buttons for zooming the current item. You can also drag the slider to the left or to the right to zoom the image.

152

Figure 81: Status bar

Status Bar—this is a bar on the very bottom of the Paint window. It shows the details of the current image on your work area. When you point to any position in your image, it measures the position for you below your work area, mostly on your left-hand side.

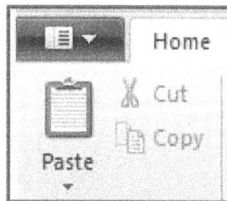

Figure 82: Paint button

Paint Button—this is like the Office Button in Office suites. You can click on it to do many things on your Paint window, or with the current image. Click on it to save, create new image, save as, print, or do anything else with your current image (See above).

Figure 83: Work area in Paint

Work area—this is a place where you work with images, and other items. You can change the size of the selected work area, using the marks indicated above. Clicking and dragging each mark changes

153

the size of the selected image, vertically or horizontally. Using the marks shown above is not recommended, because you will create blank areas in the picture, or you will lose some parts of the picture, if you zoom or squeeze the picture. Better use the (+) and (-) signs to zoom your picture (See zoom slider above).

CHAPTER 3: MAKING BOOK COVERS WITH PAINT

~~**~~

There are many ways to create a book cover. One way to make a book cover is to use CreateSpace/KDP Cover Creator templates, where you can edit those templates using Paint. Another way to make a book cover is taking a screenshot (of your computer screen), and then edit it, using Paint. When you are making a book cover for eBooks, you can use the latter option, but when you make a cover for the print book, you have to have a frame (measurement) for the cover before painting it with Paint.

Creating a cover for an eBook with Paint

To make an eBook cover, you have to use another tool called Snipping Tool, which is part of the Windows Operating Systems. To open this tool, click **Start Button**, type "**Snipping Tool,**" and then click on its icon to open it. If you cannot see the tool, click "**All Programs,**" link, click **Accessories**, and then click "**Snipping Tool,**" icon to open it. Make sure you are on the desktop view of your computer, meaning no other open windows. You can now carefully draw a picture of your eBook by taking/snipping a part of your desktop, using the tool. Left-click the desktop, as you hold down the left-mouse button, drag the mouse pointer from left to right, and then move it downward, just as you want your new e-book cover to look (size). Then release the mouse button and save the picture on your desktop for quick access. It is your choice to save the image in any place, but remember that place, so that you do not forget it. Now, open the saved image with your default image program and then open the same image in Paint. For you to follow me well, I have decided to do the process for you practically, so that you can learn by doing. Let us begin creating a real e-book cover now, using Paint.

Using Snipping Tool to capture an image

Below is the snipped image from my desktop. I will polish the image and make it into an e-book cover. Remember, an e-book cover has only one side (front).

Figure 84: Captured eBook image

This is the image for my e-book cover. Now, let me save the image and then open it in Paint, so that I can begin painting. I will use Paint to enter text into the above picture, and I will change colours. I will discover many Paint features as we polish the above e-book cover. You can do the same thing. Capture your screen as shown above, and then use the save button on snipping tool to save the file.

Opening the image in Paint and polishing it

Now, locate the saved file wherever you saved and open it using your default program for opening image files. I recommend **Windows Photo Viewer**, because it has an option to open the same file in Paint. If not, right click on the image, and then click the "Open with..." option to choose Paint. When the image is opened in Paint, it will look like the one below. You may need to resize the Paint window to see the whole picture.

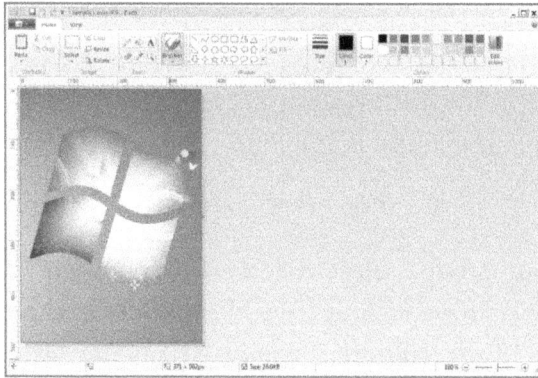

Figure 85: Editing in Paint

You can see our image now opened in Paint for editing and painting. We will use the tools mentioned above to polish the picture, and make it into an e-book cover that will look nice to the eye. People still judge the book by its cover.

Let us polish the image now. The first thing I will do after this is to change the general colour/background colour for the image, using my favourite colour.

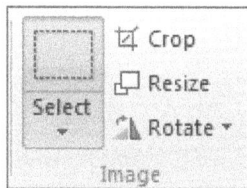

Figure 86: Image tools

To change the background colour, I have to use the "**Select**," command found under "**Image**," tab group under the "**Home tab**," in Paint. To select the whole image, click on the little arrow on the "**Select button**," and then choose "**Select all**," option as shown above.

157

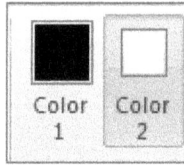

Figure 87: Two colours

In the colour group, select the secondary colour (2) and then choose your favourite colour from the colours in the ribbon. You can use the "**Edit colours,**" command on the far right to add colours that are not displayed here by default (Figure 79). After selecting your colour, just hit the "**Delete,**" button on your keyboard, and the selected area of the image will be in your selected colour. You may need to select different parts of the image differently until you are sure your colour has been applied in the whole image as shown below.

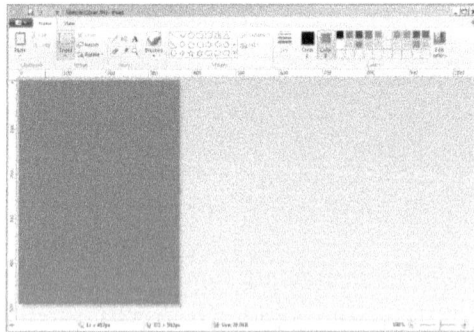

Figure 88: Background options

As you can see above, that is my colour. Now, let us enter the title of the book, and other required information such as the sub-title and author name. I will use the tools group to add text to the image above.

Figure 89: Text tools

As you can see above, I will use the "**A**" button to add text into my image.

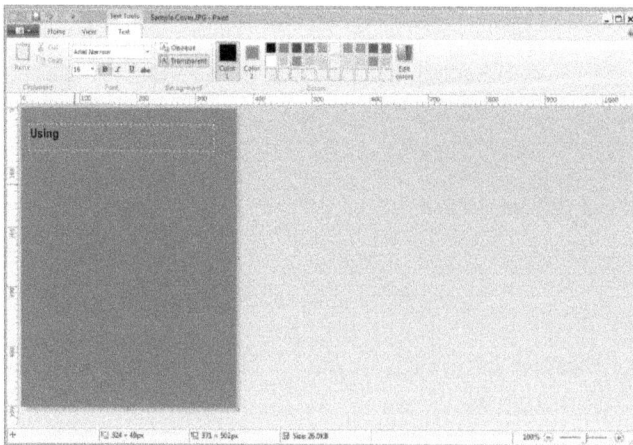

Figure 90: Inserting text into image

As you can see above, I began entering the text for the title of the book. Creativity is highly needed here. The text box must be moved, resized, and formatted in different ways, depending on the painter. Below is my full painting work for this cover, using text, and colours on Paint. When a new item is selected, new tabs also appear. When you are using text, the text tab appears on the menu bar above the ribbon as shown above.

You can choose to make the text transparent, or make it opaque. I love using the first (transparent). You have to be creative here, to design your own cover the way you like. Creativity is not about the tools in use; rather, it is about what the creator has in mind.

159

I am here to show only the simple procedures to take when making your own e-book covers, using simple tools, Microsoft Paint.

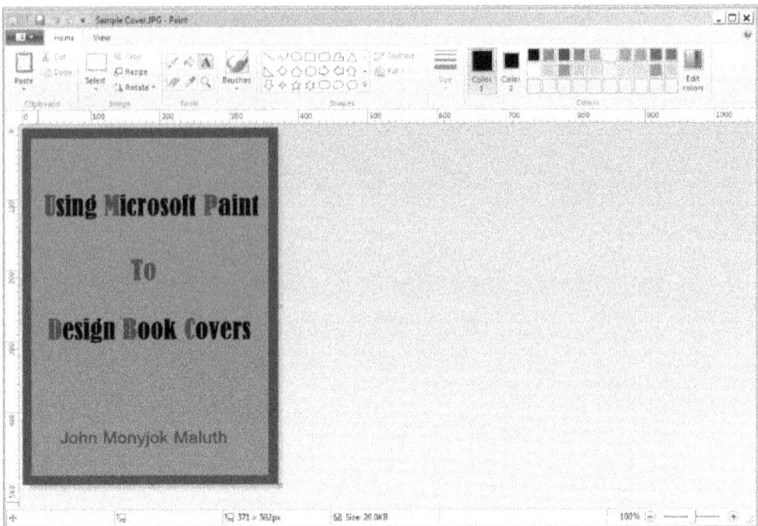

My current image (e-book) sample is, "**Using Microsoft Paint To Design Book Covers**," but yours may look different. This image was an e-book cover of this guide you are reading. Now, save your work in Paint before you close the program. Be careful when entering text, because when you click outside the text box, you will have to create another text box since you cannot edit the text.

Resizing images in Paint

One important thing you must know after creating the image for an e-book cover is its pixels. Most platforms support 300 DPI, and if your picture is less than 300 DPI, (Dot per Inch), chances are that your cover will not meet the recommended submission requirements of your platform. Smashwords recommend a cover with at least 1,600 x 2400 dimensions. How do I resize the pixels for the image? Follow the steps below. Under the image tab group

160

in Paint, click the "Resize," button mostly found between the crop and rotate commands. The window as the one below will appear.

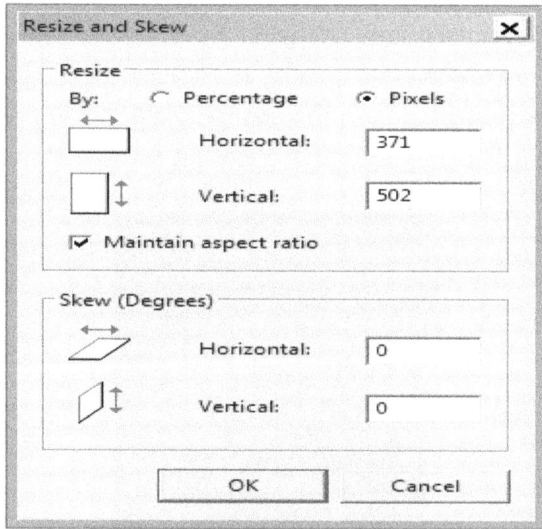

Figure 92: Resizing cover size

You can see there are two things here; resize and skew (Degrees). We are using the resize button in our case, because we want to increase the pixels of the picture. Select the radio button for pixels on the top-right of the dialogue box as shown above, and then enter the horizontal numbers and the vertical numbers. This will change the corresponding numbers, automatically. To avoid this, uncheck the "Maintain aspect ratio," and then enter the numbers manually instead.

Images with few pixels appear blurry when viewed online or when printed on paper. When done, click the **OK** button and your image size will change immediately. Save and close Paint when done. Our picture above is 371 x 502 pixels and we have to resize it to 1,600 x 2,164 pixels, so that the picture can appear clear and clean on the web.

For a print cover, we need at least 7,500 x 10,148 pixels for the best print quality. When you enter the pixels in the horizontal field, the other field will change, automatically. Press the enter key on the keyboard to preview the changes. Your picture may look very funny after increasing the pixels. It is okay, don't panic! Simply click the save button to save the changes. When you open the same cover image using any other image viewer, it will look just fine.

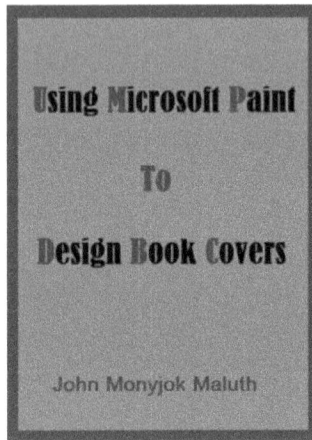

Figure 93: My e-Book Cover

This is the complete picture above for the e-book cover. Now, this image can be uploaded to Smashwords platform with no problems, because it has passed the submission requirement test. As mentioned earlier, e-books only have one-sided image like this. However, when creating a print book cover, you have to measure the cover against the page numbers of the book. You have to do some math in order to get started.

Creating the Paperback book cover with Paint

First, we have to determine the size of our book before we create a cover for it. We can either calculate the size of our book or use a template from a company such as CreateSpace. First, let us use what we have. Below, we are going to use almost the same procedures used above to create a print book cover, but the paperback cover must have the front and back sides. It must have a place for spine, depending on the size of the book. If a book has about 150 pages, it must have text on the spine (glue area).

Capturing an image with Snipping Tool

Again, we have to capture a portion of our desktop screen to make a book cover image for our paperback book. As we did for an e-book cover above, we have to run the Snipping Tool by clicking Start Button => All Programs => Accessories => Snipping Tool. Now, we have to position the mouse pointer on the portion that we want to capture on the desktop, and then we can draw a picture of our paperback book.

Figure 94: Snipping Tool on Taskbar

When the Snipping Tool is pinned to the Taskbar, it looks like the one above. Simply click on its icon to open it. When it runs, you can use it to choose different snipping options, using its new button. Now, let us capture the screen for making the cover of our paperback or hardcover book.

Figure 95: Captured Paperback Cover Image

You can see above that the paperback cover is twice the size of an e-book cover, because we have to divide it into two sections. The left hand side will be for the back cover, the middle part will be for the spine, and the right hand side will be for the front cover of our print book. Nevertheless, for you to come up with the cover size, you have to calculate the spine based on the type of paper that you want to use when printing your book.

The black and white book has a different cover setting than that of a full colour book cover with bleed. Read more examples below for better understanding, or go to CreateSpace cover creating posts at CreateSpace.com (Now moved to KDP) and read more from there. You may also download the cover template for your book at CreateSpace.com (Now closed).

Below we are going to build the print book cover using Paint. You can build the cover using Cover Creator free online (KDP), if you want to do so. Are you ready to use Cover Creator? Click Cover Creator and start learning by practice right now. You can find this under the Bookshelf tab, under Content menu when you logon to your Kindle Direct Publishing platform at www.kdp.amazon.com.

Adding text to the captured image

We have to open that image in Paint in order for us to add text to it. Before adding text, we must measure the cover based on the size of our book and the quality of the paper we need the book to be printed on. I have chosen the black and white for this book as an example.

Figure 96: Editing Paperback cover in Paint

Using the selection tool on Paint, I have to select the barcode area, spine area, and the left and right sides of the image for placing a text for front and back covers, as you will see below. This book cover is for a book of 100 pages (spineless). This means there will be no title or author name on the spine, since the spine area is very small. This is how the calculation works.

The spine width for black and white-interior books

White paper: multiply the page count by **0.002252**
Cream paper: multiply the page count by **0.0025**

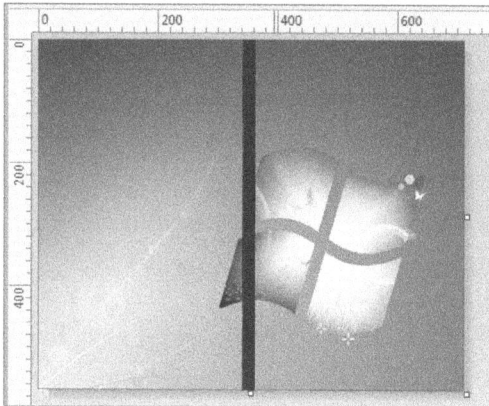

Figure 97: Locating the spine

The centre of the image above is indicated by the square mark as shown above. I have marked the pine of the book even though the book is spineless based on its' number of pages. On the left, I will enter the text for the back cover, such as about the author text, leave the barcode area blank and then enter the text for back cover text. On the right, I will enter the text for the book title, author name and subtitle. The book is 100 pages big, times 0.002252 = 0.2252 spine width because it is going to be printed in black and white on white paper. You can see how small our spine area is going to be. That is why we have a spineless cover image as you can see below.

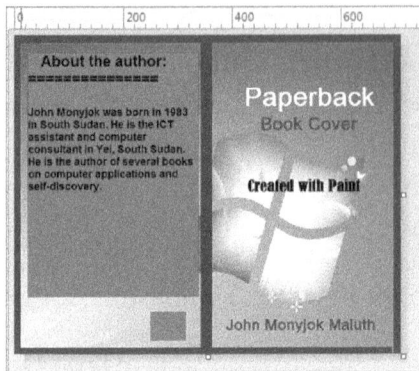

Figure 98: Finishing Paperback cover editing

You can see the paperback book cover now as shown in the picture above. This is just a sample, and that is why I did not remove the Windows Logo image that was captured with the image. The red rectangular area on the left is for the barcode area. I can add the author photo when needed, just on the left-hand side, the back cover. I can add a picture to the right hand side of the picture, if I wanted, also known as a front cover image.

Before saving, we have to check the DPI of this cover for our paperback book. If the book is going to be printed on CreateSpace/KDP, then we must use CreateSpace/KDP's DPI requirements that are 300 DPI and above. To check the DPI, I have to click the **"Resize,"** button on Paint.

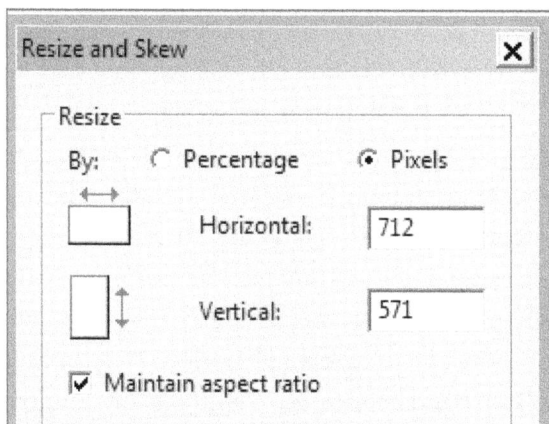

Figure 99: Resizing Paperback cover image

Wow! Good quality image is here. We have 712 DPI measurements for this cover as you can see above. The Dot per Inch is a measurement of pixels per a picture vertically and horizontally. To change the length and widths of the picture independently, **uncheck** the "Main aspect ratio" button. This will not resize the inches for our 6 x 9 measurements, but it will change the quality of the image for the best printing appearance. Since 712 is higher than the cover submission requirement of CSP (300 DPI), we cannot change this now. To submit this cover to CS/KDP platform, I have to convert it into a Portable Document Format (PDF). The system will check the design issues, and if the cover passed the submission requirements, then I will receive a message from CSP/KDP in about 24 hour's time from the time this cover was submitted. If there are any issues, I will have to fix them and then resubmit the same cover for review by CSP/KDP Team.

Recommendations

In this book, you have learned how to design e-book covers, using Paint and the Snipping Tool. These tools are all part of any Windows operating system. They are easy to use. I use them often because first, I could not afford the professional cover designers and I could not use more complicated tools such as Adobe

Photoshop. Even if one can use Photoshop, the question is; can you get one? You have to buy Photoshop in order to use it for long. What if you cannot buy it for whatever reasons? In South Sudan during the time when this book was written, it was still a dream to buy things online. You need a credit card to buy things online, and that card must be secure. It is not easy getting one because most banks in South Sudan have not even had the services like these when this book was written. However, with our free tools, we can create a professional book cover, both for e-books and paperbacks. If you cannot use Paint and the Snipping tool, you can still use CreateSpace/KDP Cover Creator online.

When submitting your book files for publication, CSP/KDP system asks you to either upload your PDF cover image or use the Online Cover Creator, free. I personally started my publishing career using these free tools until I could pay for the paid services such as the Expanded Distribution. It cost $25.00 to buy the EDC because it can expose your book to many online shoppers and retailers such as Baker & Taylor, Online Libraries and more.

I recommend Paint, if you cannot hire someone to design your book covers for you. Amazon Kindle Direct Publishing has a cover creator for free just similar to the CSP Cover Creator, and you can make use of this tool as well. If you have published books with KDP, then you already know about this beta tool. If you can afford a cover creator for a fee, then that is the best option for you, but this guide, like other guides is for those who cannot afford paying for any service.

I was once in such a situation, but KDP and CSP helped me out of the problem. Now, I can pay for services that are very important for me. If you love our services, you can also see our costs below for each book design and publishing. We will design your book covers, both for print and e-book formats as you suggest. We will then publish the book for you. If your book is in an e-book format, then you will only pay for design and formatting services. To get royalties for your book after publication, you have to create a free account with Payoneer, so that we send you your royalties using that MasterCard.

Please check all these in details below for better understanding and decision-making. If you can do your own designing, editing, converting, publishing, and marketing, that is great. This is the heart of my writings. I want all my readers to do what I can do, themselves. However, in case they cannot do the same for whatever reasons, I can then step in to help them as they pay an affordable fee. You can download the cover template from the CSP website, if you want. However, you have to follow their guidelines very carefully, as you edit your image in **Paint** or in your favourite image editor, such as Adobe Photoshop, if you have one.

DISCIPLESHIP PRESS PRICES

E-book Design Prices

With e-books, you only pay for the design (cover and interior), editing, converting, proofreading, publishing, and marketing that we will do for you. Publishing your book on KDP or Smashwords is free, but we convert your book files into Kindle format, which is not free. See the prices here for Kindle formatting.

It is even harder to convert your book according to Smashwords Submission Requirements, especially if you wrote your book using the latest Microsoft Office programs. See the Smashwords Style Guide for more information on how you can do this hard work. If you can do the work, then that is great. However, if you cannot do it, we are here to help you for a fee. With Smashwords, your book will be in multiple formats such as ePub, Kindle, Pdf, plain text and more. Bear in mind that anyone can buy your book and use it as his own (no Digital Rights Management).

Notice: If your book contains pictures, you will have to consider a different price, not listed here. We will contact you about this during the publication process. Write to maluthabiel@gmail.com.

E-book Cover Design Prices

In case you have decided to publish your own book, but you could not design your cover, we are here to help. However, if you can publish your book on KDP or Smashwords, chances are that you can design your book cover too! Nevertheless, if you cannot, just let us know using the address above, so that we discuss the prices for this service. The costs will depend on the size, quality and the type the book you have.

Paperback Cover Design Prices

If you cannot design your own paperback or hardcover book, we are here to help you. I also believe that if you can use Lulu or CreateSpace to publish your paperback book, you can also use the Cover Creator to create book covers. However, in case you cannot, we are here to help. The professional cover design by CreateSpace costs from $300.00 to $1,300, depending on what type of cover you chose! We will do the same job for you. However, our covers may not be the same as those of CreateSpace. Therefore, you will pay less than the given prices above. Depending on the size and the design type, you will pay about $100.00 or less.

Interior Book Design Prices

Books must be in a certain design format, not only on the cover, but also on the inside part, the book interior. Whether your book is an e-book or paperback, it you must format in a certain way. There are two types of paragraphs in the interior designing. The first paragraphing is **block** and the other is **indented**. The headings in a book should appear in certain ways. The font face, font size and other styles must look professional. I used the first type when writing this book: block. The genre of your book matters the most. A history book is always written in prose, not in poetical tone or language. The book you are reading is formatted as prose, not as poetic book. The margins flow from left to right, also known as **justify**, using word processors, such as OpenOffice and Microsoft Word. However, in case the tone of the book changes for whatever reasons, the format of that part must also change. Poetic text is formatted differently: centred.

If you can professionally design your book's interior, then that is what I want. If not, we are here to help, for a fee. Just let us know using the details below. You can download the cover templates for your book on CreateSpace/KDP website (Removed). You can also download the interior file templates for your book, especially when you are a beginner, or new in the world of independent publishing. Contact us below for help.

Email us now at <u>maluthabiel@gmail.com</u> or call us at +254 797 624 994 or with +211 927 145 394 or +211 910 695 304.☐

BOOK 5: MICROSOFT WORD 2007

Introduction to Microsoft Word 2007 Guide

Microsoft Word is simply a word processing program. We use it for creating documents such as reports, assignments, class notes, and other types of documents. You need word to type your assignments. I used Word for writing this very book.

The main reason for me to compile this guide is to help you use this program easily. You need to know the main features of the program, but you will only learn through practice. Bear in mind that, as technology grows, things begin to change.

In this book, we will use Microsoft Office Word 2007. There are many versions of Microsoft Office. There is Office 2003, 2007 (this version), 2010 and Office 2013. I will compare Office 2007 and 2010 in this book, so that if you use the other, you will not be left wondering. I personally love using Office 2007.

Remember, there are many great programs in any Office version. We have Access, Excel, Groove, InfoPath, OneNote, Outlook, PowerPoint, Publisher, and Word. You may not necessary need to know how to use all these programs. You may use some of them, depending on what you want to do with your computer. If you really master Office Word program, you are well off. You can even use Word to create good-looking certificates! In this book, we are going to look at the main features of Word. When I use "Word," I mean the Microsoft Office Word program in whatever version you may be using right now. Microsoft Word is also known as MS Word in short. I love this tool. I use it all the time for doing many things. I use it to write and design books, do office work, assignments, reports, and other documents. The main tabs in Word are, Home, Insert, Page Layout, Reference, Mailings, Review, and View. Nevertheless, when you are working with pictures or textboxes, you will see the "Format" or **Drawing Tools** tabs, added to the menu bar.

Let's get going!

CHAPTER 1: HOME TAB

~~**~~

Introduction

In this chapter, we are going to look at the Clipboard, Font, Paragraph, Styles and Editing tab groups. All these tab groups are under the "**Home Tab**," and you can use them to make a professional document. This Home Tab is what you will use all the time to format your work the way you want. There are different commands under each tab group, represented by icons. You will have to click these icons to do your work.

1. Click **Start Button**.
2. Click "**All Programs**."
3. Click "**Microsoft Office**" folder.
4. Click "**Microsoft Office Word**."

Clipboard Group

This tab group is on the far right corner of your open Word window. To access MS Word program, please see those steps above. You can also left-click the Microsoft Office Word icon, if you can see it on the Start Menu. Check **Windows 7 For Beginners** (**Part I**) for more information about how to work with Windows. In that book, you will learn that there are different ways of opening a program in Windows.

If the program is on the Taskbar, left-click on its icon. Now, you can continue the learning process by checking the clipboard group. On the clipboard tab group, you will find commands like, cut, copy, and paste. To cut means to remove the selected item completely from where it is right now. To paste means to place the cut item to the new location or place. The difference between copy and cut is that when you copy an item, it is not removed completely from the current location. You can still paste the copied or cut items to a new location as you wish.

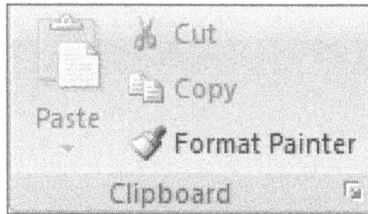

Figure 100: Clipboard Tab Group

If a command icon is dim, it means there is no need to use it at this time. As you can see in the picture above, the cut, paste, and copy commands are dim, because there is nothing in my clipboard right now. However, if I selected any object in the document, the cut and copy command icons will be active. If I copied or cut the selected text, the paste command will also be active. That diagonal arrow on the far right-bottom of the clipboard group area can be used to open the clipboard pane.

The "**Format Painter**," button is used to apply your current format to different parts of your document. Double-click on this button to see what to do with this command. There are different pasting commands such as, paste, paste special, or paste as hyperlink.

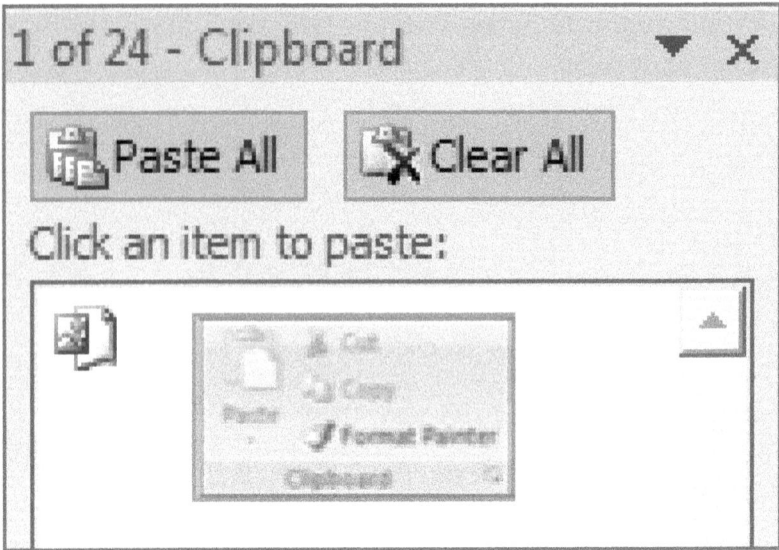

Figure 101: Clipboard items

To see what is on your clipboard, click on the diagonal arrow in the clipboard tab group, and the dialogue box like the one above will appear on the left side of the screen. You can either paste all into your document, or clear them all from the clipboard area. Use the little arrow next to the close button to setup your clipboard pane window.

You can use the close button to close the clipboard pane window just like any other window. If you look to the bottom of the clipboard pane window, you will see a button that says, "**Options,**" with an arrow next to it. Click this button to do more settings with your clipboard pane window.

Now, let us move on to other tab groups under the Home Tab in Microsoft Word program. In addition, you can click an item in the clipboard pane window and then paste it into your document.

Tips and tricks

Cut—to cut an item select it, and then use Ctrl+X to cut it and keep it in the clipboard area for a while. The item will be there until you shut down your computer.

Copies—to copy an item select it, and then use Ctrl+C to copy it and keep it in the clipboard area for a while. The item will be there until you shut down your computer.

Paste—to paste an item that you have cut or copied, use the Ctrl+V to paste it into the new location quickly with no delay. I use these commands every day. They become part of my daily computing tasks.

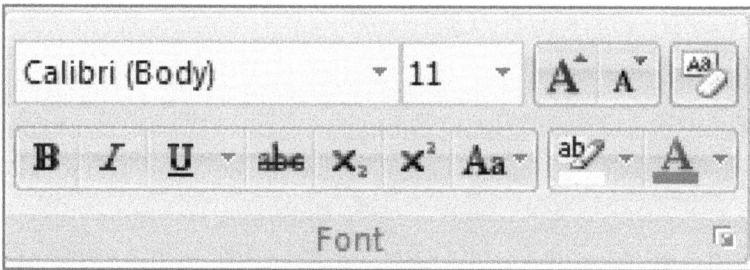

Figure 102: Font Group

Font Group

Under this tab group, we will look at Font face, Colour Size, Text Highlight Colour, and Clear Formatting. We will also look at other important commands. We will look at the **Bold**, *Italic*, and Underline commands. You will also learn about commands such as Strikethrough, Subscript, Superscript, Change Case, Grow Font, and Shrink Font. In addition, there is a diagonal arrow in this tab group as shown below.

To apply any of these formatting commands, you have to select your text first. You can use "**B**" command to **bold** the selected text, and "*I*" to make the text *Italic*. You can use the "U" command to underline the selected text. There are different ways to underline your work, and that is why you have the arrow next to the underline command. You will also need to set the font face and size. Our default font face as you can see above is "Calibri (Body), but you can change it to any font face.

To open the font face list, hit the arrow near the font face. To change the font size, hit the arrow near the font size number. Our default size is 11, as you can see above. To quickly increase or decrease font size, select your text and then use the Grow or Shrink Font commands by left-clicking them. You can use the "**Change Case**," command to change from UPPER to lower cases. You can also use the Sentence Case, Toggle Case, or just Capitalize Each Word in the selected line of text. You can also select the text and then click on the font colour command button to apply the colour.

Our default colour is red, but you can use the arrow next to the font/text colour to show more colours in the list. To open the font dialogue box, click on the diagonal arrow in the Font Tab group, using the left mouse button, left-clicking. To remove any formatting of your text, left-click on the "**Clear Formatting**," button once. You will have to select the formatted text before you can remove the formatting.

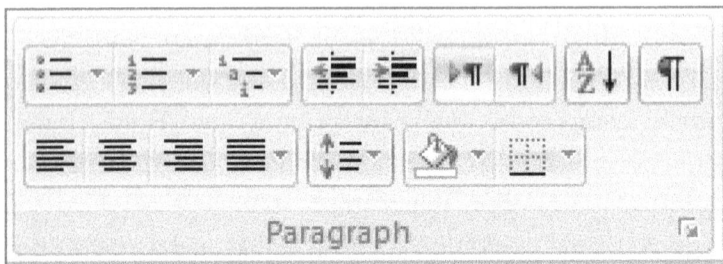

Figure 103: Paragraph group

Paragraph Group

Under the Paragraph Tab Group, you can find commands to align your text to the right, left centre or justified. You can also find commands that will add bullets and numbers to your text. You can do a lot of text formatting here.

To align the text to your desired location, just select it and then click on the command you want to apply. You can align text or picture in your document to the right, left, centre or justify it. To justify an item means you make it fit to the work area on both left and right sides. Use this command to format your text to look the same on the right and left sides of the screen.

You can use text direction from right to left or from left to right. You can set the space between the lines of text, or add a space between paragraphs. You can paint or share the background of any selected text or paragraph, using the theme colours. You can decrease or increase the indentation of your work. This will move the text in or out of the margins. You can also use bordering to put a line under or on top of the selected text. You can sort your work numerically or alphabetically. You can show/hide the paragraph markings using the show/hide button.

Formatting Buttons

Use this button to align text or an item to the left of the work area.

Use this button to align text or an item to the centre of the work area.

Use this button to align text or an item to the right side of the work area.

Use this button to align text as "justified" and there are different ways to do this. This is why you can see a little arrow, meaning there are many other choices to make. You can justify,

justify low, justify medium or justify high. I recommend you use the first option: "justify" only.

Use this button to set the line spacing. In your academic writing assignment, you may be asked to use a certain font face, and then double-space your work. You may be told to use the 1.5 line spacing. This is where to go to choose your desired formatting.

Use this button to choose the shading colour for the selected text. You have theme and standard colours to choose from, using the small arrow next to this button as shown here.

Use this button to make borders. The default border here is "**Bottom Border**," because it can add a border on the bottom of the selected text. You can change the border type and location, using the arrow next to the command button as shown here.

Use this button to add bulleted lists to your work. There are many different kinds of bulleted list designs. Use the little arrow next to the command button to see more.

Use this button to add a number list to your lines of text. You can choose many numbering types, using a little arrow next to the command button as shown here.

Multilevel List

Use this button to add a multilevel list to your selected text. There are many types of multilevel listing, which you can also choose from, using the small arrow next to the command button as shown here.

Decrease and Increase Indent

Use these buttons to increase or decrease the indentation of your work. Clicking on either button will increase or decrease the indentation of the selected text.

Text Direction—Left to Right

Use this button to set the text direction from left to right. This default text direction in English and other languages, apart from Arabic and other languages, writes from right to left.

Text Direction—Right to Left

Use this button to change the writing direction. This is good when writing in Arabic or Hebrew.

Sorting

Use this button to sort your work alphabetically or numerically.

Show/Hide

Use this button to show or hide paragraph return formatting marks in your document.

Tips and tricks

Show/Hide—to show or hide the paragraph return formatting, use Ctrl+*, but this may not work on all keyboards.

Align Right—to align text or an item to the right, use Ctrl+R after selecting it.

Align Left—to align text or an item to the right, use Ctrl+L after selecting it.

Align Centre—to align text or an item to the centre, use Ctrl+E after selecting it.

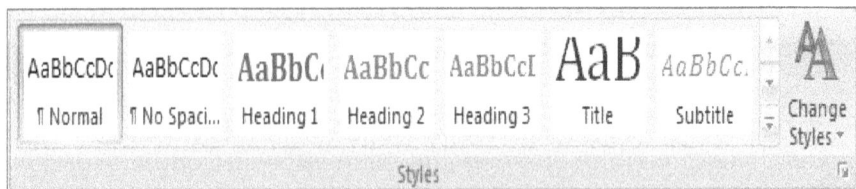

Figure 104: Styles Group

Style Group

There are many good styles in MS Word. Here you will find styles such as Normal, No Spacing, Heading 1, Heading 2, Heading 3, Title, and then Subtitle. To show many other commands under the Styles Tab group, use the arrow in the middle. To show all styles, use the arrow below, also known as "More Styles."

If you really want to create a professional looking document, you will have to use styles. Styles are good for formatting. You can use styles to create headings and other formatting styles. If you want to create a table of contents, you will use headings. The "Heading 1" style is good for book chapters. To apply a certain style to a line of text or paragraph, click on the text and then point to the style in the ribbon, to see a live preview. In our picture above, the "**Normal**," style is selected, meaning there is no special style used in my text. The "**No Spacing**," style means there will be no line spacing between the lines of text, or paragraphs when you apply this styling to your text. The "**Title**," style is good for the title of your book. There is another style for your subtitle as well.

There are many styles, and you can access them using the two arrows on the far right of the styles group as shown above. The last arrow down is to show all styles at once. The one in the middle is for showing the styles line by line. Use the upper arrow to go back to previous styles. Use the "**Change Styles,**" button on the far right of the styles tab as shown above. To do more settings on the styles, use the diagonal arrow on the bottom-right of the styles group section. You can also use the "**Change Styles,**" button to change colours, fonts, and style set. You can also save your new changes as default.

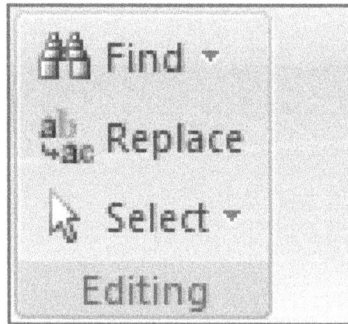

Figure 105: Editing group

Editing Group

Under this tab group, we will look at commands such as, **Find**, **Replace**, and **Select** and these are other important commands you need to know. With the **Find** Command, you can find words easily in your document. With **Replace** Command, you can find and easily replace text with another text. With the **Select** Command, you can Select All, Select Objects, or Select Text with Similar Formatting in the document.

As mentioned above, you can use the find command button to quickly find words in your document. Next to each command button, you can see a small arrow pointing downwards (Find and Select only). This arrow can be used to find other sub-commands under each command.

Clicking this arrow next to the "**Find,**" command button will reveal other commands such as, "Find...," and "Go To." You can use the

"Go To," command, to go to a section or page in the document. You can go to a page, section, line, bookmark, comment, footnote, endnote, field table, graphic, equation, object, or heading in your document. Selecting any of these commands will make you able to access other commands in one place. This means when you click on the "**Find...**," command, you will also see a link to "**Replace, and Go To**," commands on the same window that will open. Remember, there are many commands under each tab group.

Next, in chapter two, we will look at the "**Insert Tab**," in Microsoft Word 2007 program.

CHAPTER 2: INSERT TAB

~~**~~

Introduction

In this second tab, we will talk about tab groups such as **Pages, Tables, Illustrations, Links, Header & Footer, Text,** and **Symbols**. These are buttons representing other commands in the ribbon. These features are the same in most Office applications, and if you master them all in Word, then you have no problem with other Microsoft office programs. To insert means to add something into your document. You can insert pages, tables, pictures, links, headers and footers, text and symbols.

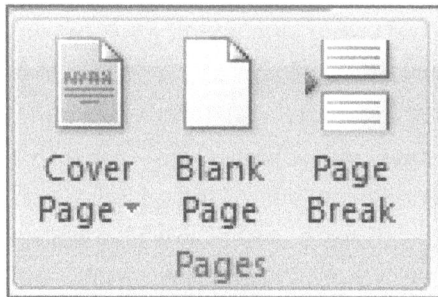

Figure 106: Pages group

Pages Group

Under pages tab group, you can insert things such as cover Page, Blank Page, and Page Break. There is a small arrow under the Cover Page command icon, and you can use this to see many other cover page styles. As mentioned earlier, you can add a cover page into your document. You can also add a blank page. You can add a page break, using the command buttons shown above. To apply a certain cover page style, simply click on it, using the left mouse button and it will apply. You can now replace the default text and other placeholder with your own text, according to your wishes.

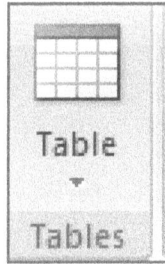

Table Group

You can also insert a table into your document, but how can you do this? You will learn how to do this shortly. You can do this by clicking on the Insert Tab in the menu bar, and then select the table under the tables tab group.

To insert a table into your document, click on the table command button as shown above, and you will see a window with little boxes on it. You will see that there are 80 boxes in number. These boxes represent cells: rows and columns. You can use these to create a new table. Depending on what kind of table you want to create, you can either use those boxes to create a table, or insert a table into the document. You can also insert or draw a table, using those commands, as they will show up as you click on the table command button. You can also use the quick table option, where you can insert a template of a table into your document. You can also convert text to a table, but you have to select the text first for this button to be active. You can also insert an Excel Spreadsheet into your document. Be informed that Excel Program will open.

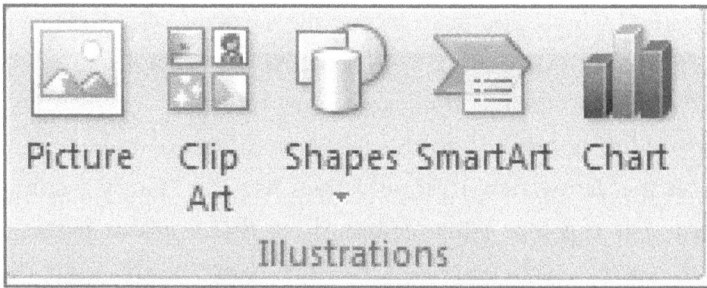

Illustrations Group

Under illustrations, you can insert Pictures, Clip Art, Shapes, Smart Art, and Charts. However, how can you do this? You can do this by clicking on the Insert Tab, and then look for these commands in the illustration section as shown above.

To insert a picture or any other object to illustrate a point in your document, click on its associated command as shown above. To insert a picture into your document, click on the "**Picture,**" command button, and a open file dialogue box will open. Now, select a picture from your computer and then click on the "**Insert,**" button on that window to insert the picture into your document. First, you have to click on the area in your document where you want the picture to appear.

To insert a Clip Art into your document, click on its command button, and a pane will open on the right hand side of your window. Here, you can see buttons such as, "Organize clips... Clip Art on Office Online, and Tips for finding clips. The first button is what you need for now. It is called, "Organized clips...," and you can click there to open your clips. When you clicked there, a window will open in the middle of your computer screen. On this window, you will see a collection list where you can find different pictures. The default collections are, My Collections, Office Collections, and Web Collections. Under My Collections, you will see other sub-collections such as Favourites Clips and the

Unclassified Clips. You have to use the Office Collections to insert clips into your document. You will discover that there are other clips categories when you clicked here. Use Web Collections only when you are connected to the Internet. When you like a clip, just click on the arrow new to it, and then use the "**Copy**," command to copy that clip into your clipboard, so that you can paste it into your document. When done, close the pane on the right part of your window. To learn the tricks of pasting, see clipboard tab group above (Figure 106).

To insert shapes into your document, click on the shapes command button as shown above, and you will see all kinds of shapes. Shapes are Lines, Basic Shapes, Block Arrows, Flowcharts, Callouts, Stars, and Banners. You can also use New Drawing Canvas, if you are good with drawing. To add a shape, click on it once, and then draw it on your document. This means you will have to use your left-mouse button to click as you drag the mouse pointer to a desired position.

To insert a SmartArt, click on the SmartArt command button, and a window will open where you will see many graphics. These graphics are organized in sections such as **All**, **List**, **Process**, **Cycle**, **Hierarchy**, **Relationship**, **Matrix**, and **Pyramid**. There are many shapes under each section, and you can see them when you selected the group heading.

To insert charts, click on the chart command button. You can choose charts such as, **Column**, **Line**, **Bar**, **Pie**, **Area**, **Surface** and many more from many chart categories. Use these chart types to illustrate and compare data on your document.

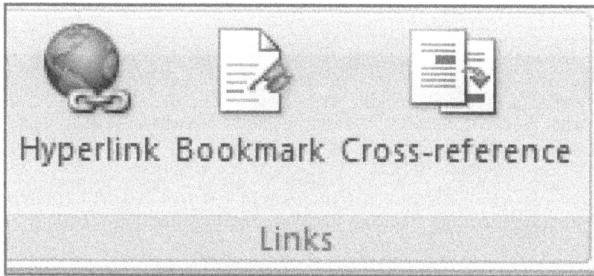

Links Group

Here, you can insert hyperlinks, bookmarks, and cross-references into your documents. If you are a book editor, or an indie author, you need to know how to insert links and bookmarks into your book. To insert a hyperlink into a text, select the text and then click on the hyperlink command button. A dialogue box will open where you have to choose where to get the link. You can link to an existing file or webpage, place in this document, create a new document that you can link to, or link to an email address. You can also look in the current folder, browsed pages or recent files to link to. If you want to link to a bookmark or heading in the same document, then use the place in this document option. You can also type a text to display, if you want, and then click the **Ok** button when done, to close the dialogue box.

To insert bookmarks, you have to click on the bookmark command button as shown above. Remember to type a name of the bookmark. A bookmark name must not begin with a number or a special character. It must be one word or words, typed as one word, no spacing between them. You can also insert a cross-reference from the same document. To do this, click on the cross-reference command button, and a window will open where you will select what to link to the document, and then click the **Insert** button in that window. You can insert a numbered item, heading, bookmark, footnote and more.

189

Header & Footer Group

Here, you can insert headers & footers to your document. You can insert a page number as well, if you want to. Headers are placed on the top part of your pages, while footers are placed on the bottom part. There are four heading & footing styles, which you can choose from. You can edit, remove, or save selection to header or footer gallery. You can insert, format or remove page numbers.

To insert a header text into your document, click the **"Header,"** command button as shown above, and choose the type you like among the four types. To insert a footer text into your document, click on the **"Footer,"** command button as shown above, and choose from the four types of text styles. To insert a page number, click on the **"Page Number,"** command button as shown above. You will choose whether you want to insert the number on top, bottom or into the margins/left or right. You can insert a page number on the top of the page, and align it to the centre, left or right, with different styles.

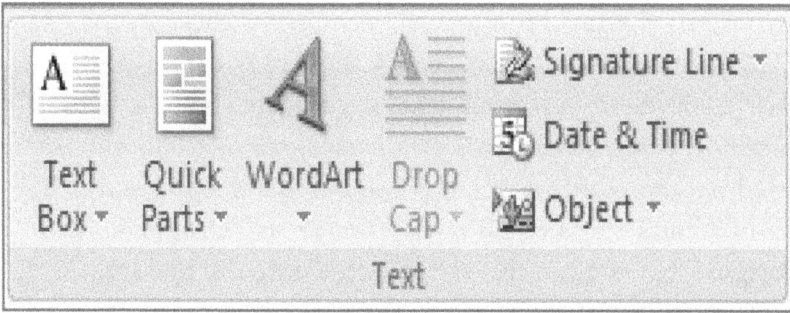

Figure 111: text group

Text Group

Under the text tab group, you can insert into your document a Textbox, Quick Parts, WordArt, Drop Cap, Signature Line, Date & Time and finally, an Object. How can you do this? Read on and find out how as discussed below.

To insert a textbox into your document, click on the "**Text Box**," command button. There are preformatted text templates boxes that you can choose from. You can even draw a text box. When done, you can save that selection to the textbox gallery for future use.

To insert quick parts into your document, click "**Quick Parts**," command button, and choose from the list of many things you can add to your document. You can add the author, abstract, category and comments under the "**Document Properties**," section. You can also insert a field or building blocks organizer into your document. When done, you can choose to save the selection to the Quick Part Gallery for your future use, if you want to do that.

To insert a WordArt, click on the "**WordArt**," command button as shown above. You can also select the text in your document, then click on the WordArt command button, and then choose from the long list of styles available. A dialogue box will appear where you can do a lot more settings to your WordArt style before you press the **Ok** button to apply it to your document.

To insert a Drop Cap into your document, click on the "**Drop Cap**," command button as shown above. Of course you have to click somewhere near your text before you click the Drop Cap button. If you click or move your cursor to a new line with no text typed yet, the WordArt or Drop Cap buttons will be inactive. There are two quick styles of Drop Cap known as "**Dropped**," and "**In Margin**," but you can also choose more drop cap options.

You can insert the date and time into your document using the "**Date & Time**," command button as shown above. You can also insert an object such as the Excel Worksheet into your document. You can also insert a signature line, using the Microsoft Office Signature Lines, but you will have to fill the form before you insert it. You will be taken to the Internet, if you choose to add signature services from the list.

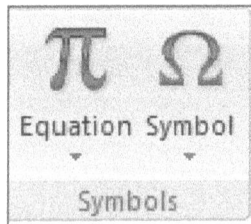

Figure 112: Symbols group

Symbols Group

This is the last tab group under the **Insert Tab**. Here, you can insert equations and symbols into your document. How can you do this?

To insert an equation symbol into your document, click the "**Equation**," command button as shown above. You have to type or select the equation symbol from the list that will appear in the ribbon, if you click on the button directly. If you clicked on the small arrow below the equation command, then you will see different equations such as the area of circle, binomial theorem and many more. Choose what you want by left-clicking it, and it will be added into your document.

To insert a symbol into your document, click on the "**Symbol**," command button. If you clicked directly on the symbol command button, you will see the recently used symbols in the list that will appear. Click on a symbol that you want to insert, and it will be inserted. You can also click on the "More Symbols..." link to see more symbols. When you get a symbol you are looking for, just select it and then click on the insert button on that window, and the symbol will be inserted. You will have to close the window in order for you to see the inserted symbol. You may keep inserting it several times, when you have already inserted the same symbols, if you still have the window open, and you may not notice this.

CHAPTER 3: PAGE LAYOUT TAB

~~**~~

Introduction

Welcome to the third chapter of this great book. This chapter is about the **Page Layout Tab** in Microsoft Word 2007 program. As you can recall, the features in MS Word Program look alike with other office programs. Under this tab, we will look at many different tab groups such as, **Themes**, **Page Setup**, **Page Backgrounds, Paragraph**, and **Arrange** tab groups. These tab groups are made up of different command buttons that represent different commands the computer will take when clicked.

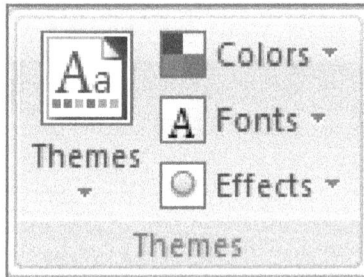

Figure 113: Themes Group

Themes Group

Under this tab group, we will discuss the themes, colours, fonts, and effects. Here, you can browse for themes, save the current theme, look for more themes on the Microsoft Office themes online, or reset to theme from template. You can choose from many themes. You can choose a colour or create your new theme colours, if you want. You can choose from many other fonts or create your new theme fonts. You can also choose from many available theme effects. The arrow next to each command button/icon in the picture above means there are many other commands under it. When you clicked on the themes command button, you will see a list of many preformatted themes that you can choose from. These themes have their own colour schemes. You can also select a new them colour, using the "**Colours**," command button as shown above. You can create your new theme colours, or choose from the existing ones, and apply it into your document. You can also choose fonts, effects or create new ones yourself, using their command buttons as shown in the picture.

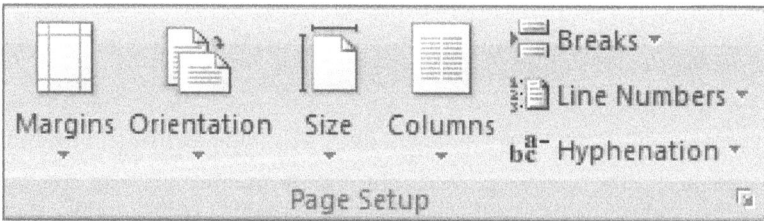

Figure 114: Page Setup Group

Page Setup Group

Under Page Setup tab group, you can set the Margins, Orientation, Size, and number of columns. You will need these settings in order to make a booklet out of the Microsoft Word program. This is why this book is good, not only for those learning about computers, but for writers as well. You will have to master these things, if you want to learn how to format/design your book's interior. This book is also great for indie authors/self-publishers. You will also learn about breaks such as section breaks and page breaks. You will also learn about line numbers and hyphenation options under this tab group.

To setup your document margins, click on the "**Margins**," command button, and you will see a number of them. You can make use of the "**Custom Margin…**" to create your own margins, if you want to do that. This is why this book is great for both beginners and writers who may be familiar with some features of this computer program. It is both a guide for the learned, and for the learners.

To setup your document page orientations, click on the "**Orientation**," command button as shown above, and you will see two different orientation options. You can now set your page to landscape or portrait options, which is to show the page as vertical or as horizontal.

To setup the size of the paper for your page, click the "**Size**," command button in the ribbon, and choose from the available pages sizes. You can even create your own size, using the "**More Paper Sizes…**" link that will appear.

To setup columns in your page, click the "**Columns**," command button as shown above, and choose from the list of available columns, or create your own, using the "**More Columns…**" link that will appear.

To create a page or a column break, use the "**Breaks**," command button as shown above, and select the right action that you want to perform. You can also choose from many ways of creating breaks under that section. You do not really need the line numbering, do you? This will count all the lines in your document, and it will then number them. There are many options to choose from under the line numbering section. The hyphenation is good in a justified text, because it can add a dash at the end of the text on the far right of the page to divide long words. This can be set to automatic, manual, or to none.

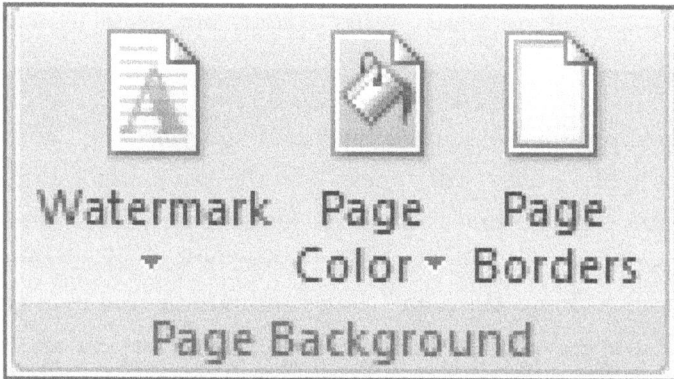

Figure 115: Page background group

Page Background Group

Under this Page Background tab group, we are discussing about **Watermark**, **Page Colour**, and **Page Borders**. You can select a watermark or remove the existing one. You can create your own watermark, or save the current one for future use. You can choose a page colour from the available colours, or create your new colours, using the "**More Colours...**" link. You can also setup the fill effects for a page colour. There are many page borders and shadings that you can choose from.

To add a watermark to your page, click the "**Watermark,**" command button as shown above, and then select one of the watermark designs you like in the list that will appear. There are two watermarks by default: **CONFIDENTIAL** and **DO NOT COPY,** all in different positions. Instead of using the preformatted watermarks, you can also use your own custom watermark by clicking on that link.

To apply a page colour, click on the "**Page Colour,**" command button as shown above, and a list of colours will appear. Just point to a colour you like, and you will see a live preview of that colour on your pages. Bear in mind that the page colour apply to all pages in your document. There are theme and standard colours. Here, you can also set the fill effects of colours. Use the "**More**

197

Colours..." link to access other colour, not listed in the quick colours' list.

To create page borders, click on the "**Page Borders**," command, and a list of borders will appear. On the same window that will open, you can also find commands for shading your selected text. To apply some shading, just select a text in your document, then click on the "**Page Borders**," command button, and then click on the "**Shading**," tab on the window that will appear. Select the colour, using the drop down menu, and then click the **OK** button, to apply it to your text. On page border and borders tab, you can use the box, shadow, 3D, or custom settings, to apply to your document. When you are done, click the **OK** button, and the border will be applied to your text. You can do more settings and apply more styles to your document, yourself.

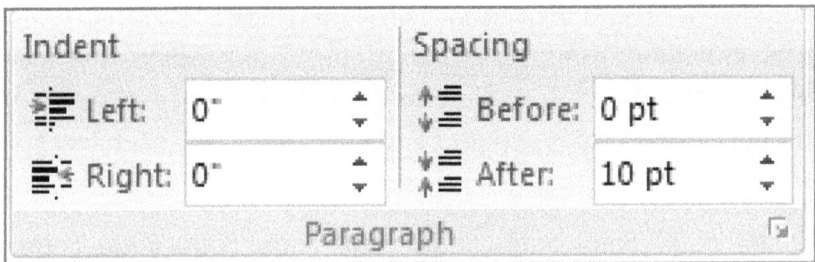

Figure 116: Paragraph Group

Paragraph Group

Under the Paragraph tab group, you can do some settings for your paragraphs. Nevertheless, there are only two main things here, the indentation, and spacing. There is also a diagonal arrow on the far right of the paragraph group where you can get to more settings, if you want. Remember, the paragraph group was also presented under the Home Tab, which is the first chapter of this book (**Part VII**). For more information about paragraphing, see chapter one.

To indent a text, use the indent section as shown in the picture above. You can use arrows to increase or decrease the indentation of text in your document. You can indent the lines on right or on the left side of the page, using the "**Left**," and "**Right**," fields as shown above. To increase the indent, use the upper arrow, and to decrease it, use the lower arrow. You have to click the arrow as many times as you want, using the left-mouse button, also known as left-clicking. To create spaces between the lines, use the "**Spacing**," section as shown above. The "**Before**," and "**After**," phrases refer to the lines between paragraphs. Mine in the picture above shows 0 pt before the line, and it shows 10 pt after the paragraph, which comes after.

To do more settings, check out the diagonal arrow on the far bottom-right of the paragraph group.

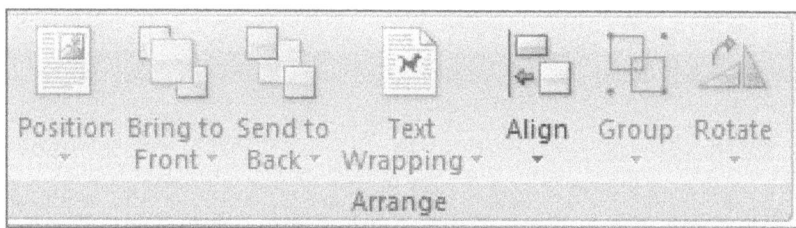

Figure 117: Arrange Group

Arrange Group

Under the **Arrange** tab group, you will learn about Position, Bring to Front, Sent to Back, Text Wrapping, Aligning, Grouping, and Rotating objects on your document. Like any other command buttons, the buttons in this section are likely to be inactive until you really need them. If you are working with text, only the "**Align**," button will be active. However, if you are working with a textbox or a picture, it is likely that other command buttons will be active. You can see in the picture above that almost all the command buttons are inactive. Can you tell why? When you do not need a command, its button will be inactive until you need it. You do not need to position a text document. You do not need to bring it to front, or send it to back. You do not need to rotate, group, or wrap it. Therefore, all those commands are appearing inactive in this picture. If I work with a text box, all these buttons will be active except the "**Group**," command button. You can only use this command to group two different objects together.

CHAPTER 4: REFERENCE TAB

~~**~~

Introduction

Welcome to the fourth chapter. We will discuss other features of Microsoft Word program such as, **Table of Contents, Footnotes, Citations & Bibliography, Captions, Index**, and **Table of Authorities**. All these sections are tab groups, and they are almost the same in all Office programs.

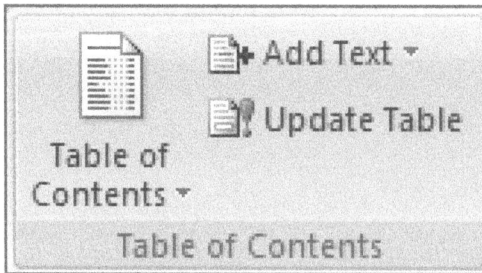

Figure 118: Table of Contents group

Table of Contents Group

Under this tab group, we will do our table of contents work. If you are a writer or a reader, then you know the importance of a table of contents in writing. A book without a table of contents can be confusing, depending on the nature of the book. Here, you will learn how to insert a table of contents to your book, or assignment in a very easy way. There are many ways to kill the rat.

As you can see in this picture above, you can add some text or update an existing table of contents. If you have no table of contents in your document, click on the **"Table of Contents,"** command button to insert one. Bear in mind that this works well if you formatted your document, using the multilevel numbering or heading styles discussed in chapter one of this book. Use the automatic way of inserting the table of contents only if you have the multilevel listing in your document, or if you have formatted your document with headings. If not, use the manual table of contents to insert your chapters and sub-chapters, manually. You can also use the "**Add Text**," command, to build your table of contents. You can also insert or remove an existing table of contents from here. To insert a table of contents, click on the command button that says, "**Insert Table of Contents...**" There you will choose to show page numbers in the table of contents or not. You will also choose the levels from a title to subtitles in your document. Click the **OK** button when you are done. This will insert a table of contents to the place of your cursor in the document.

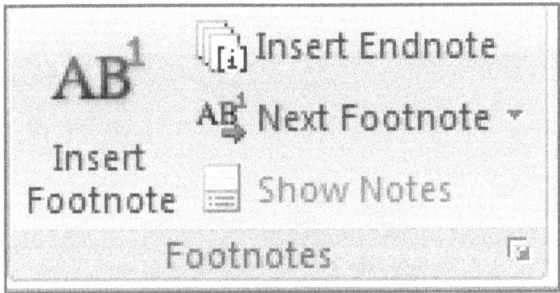

Figure 119: Footnotes group

Footnote Group

Under the Footnotes tab group, you can insert Footnotes and Endnotes into your document. If you have used someone's work in your assignment, you may need to insert a footnote into the bottom part of your document. Bear in mind that endnotes and footnotes are not the same. Endnotes are numbered, using Roman numbering, while footnotes are numbered, using the normal numbering system.

To insert a footnote, click on the "**Insert Footnote**," command button as shown in the above picture, and a number will appear in the bottom-left of your page. Here, you can enter the text about your footnote, which is always about the sources cited or quoted in your page. Each footnote is inserted on the page where the source is quoted or cited, not on the other page. Footnotes begin with number one (1), depending on the cited or quoted sources in your document.

To insert endnotes, click the "**Insert Endnote**," command button, and a Roman number will appear on the bottom-left of your document. You can also move to the next or previous endnotes or footnotes, using the "**Next Footnote**," command button with a little arrow next to it as shown above. You can also show notes, if you have them. For now, the "**Show Notes**," command button is inactive in my example, because I have no inserted notes in my document when I was writing this book. You can also use the diagonal arrow found on the far bottom-right of the footnotes tab group as shown above.

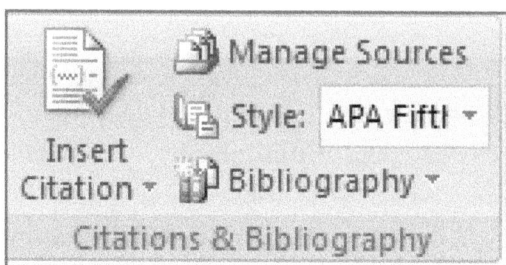

Figure 120: Citations and Bibliography

Citations & Bibliography Group

Under this tab group, you will learn how to insert Citations & Bibliographies. You will also learn how to manage sources and how to select the styles for citation and bibliography. This Reference Tab is great for academicians and students, writing academic papers. Here, you can insert citations easily into your academic paper.

To insert a citation into your work, click on the place where you want to insert it, and then click on the "**Insert Citation**," command button as shown above. You can either add a new placeholder to your document, or add a new source for citation or search libraries online. There are many different citation formats and styles that you can choose from. Bear in mind that, if you choose to search the library, a task pane will open on the right side of your window. Here, you can type a word or phrase to search for and click the "**Go**," button or press the "**Enter**," key on your keyboard. You can add a new placeholder, if you can type your own citation. To insert bibliography information into your document, click the "**Bibliography**," command button as shown above. There are many styles of bibliographies as well. First, select the style you want before you insert one.

To select a style, click on the style selector marked by the "**APA Fifth Edition**," as a default. However, you can change to any available style from the drop down menu. The APA stands for Abbreviation of Personal Allowance, or American Psychological Association.

To preview the differences between these styles, select one style, and then click on the "**Bibliography**," command button to preview it. Here, you can now insert a bibliography by selecting the style you like or click on the "**Insert Bibliography**," command that will appear. When done, you can even save the selection for your future use. You can also manage sources by adding your own new source. Remember, you cannot add a citation if you never cited anyone in your work.

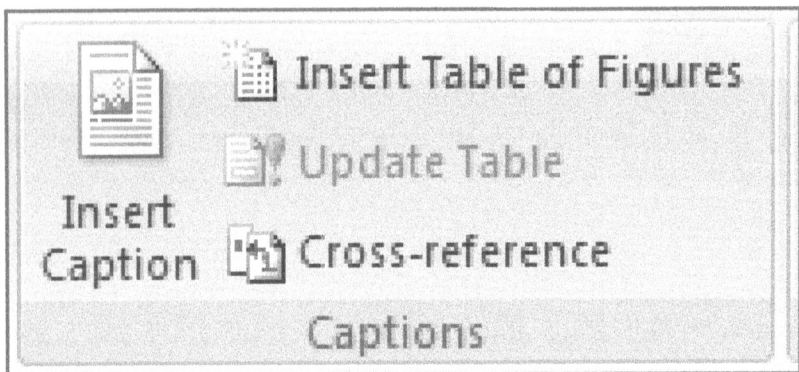

Captions Group

Under this tab groups, you can insert a table of figures, update the current tables, insert a caption, or insert a cross-reference into your document. As mentioned earlier, the whole of the "**Reference Tab**," is useful to academicians and academic students. It helps you insert academic required formatting into your documents. Captions are for figures or just descriptions of some information such as a picture in your text.

To insert a caption, click on the place where you want to insert it, and then click on the "**Insert Caption**," command button as shown above in the picture. A dialogue box will open where you will have to setup how you want your caption to look like, and then press the **OK** button to insert it.

To insert a table of figures, click on the "**Insert Table of Figures**," command button as shown above, and a window will appear. On that window, setup how you want the table to appear, and press the **OK** button to insert it. You cannot insert a table if there are no figures in your document.

To insert a cross-reference, click on the "**Cross-reference**," command button as shown above. A dialogue box will open up where you will have to setup what to connect to, and then click the "**Insert**," button on the window to insert it to the document. Learn more about the reference types in chapter 2 of this book.

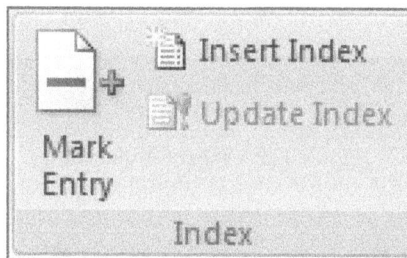

Index Group

Under this second last tab group, you can Insert Index, Mark Entry, or Update an existing index in your document. How can you do this? Read more below on how you can insert these items into your document. Remember, if a command icon or button is dim, it is inactive, and it will not work when clicked.

To mark the entry of your index, click the "**Mark Entry**," command button as shown in the above picture, and a dialogue box will open where you will setup the entry details. You will need to fill in the main entry details, and the sub-entry details, plus the options on how you want it to appear. You may need to format the page numbering as well, right on that window that will appear. You can mark as many entries as you can, while the dialogue box is open.

To insert an index, click on the "**Insert Index**," command button as shown above. Select the index type and click on the "**OK**," button. You will discover that there are many different formats of index. Use the "**Update Index**," command button to update an existing index list. Nevertheless, if you have no index entries, the button will be inactive as you can see above.

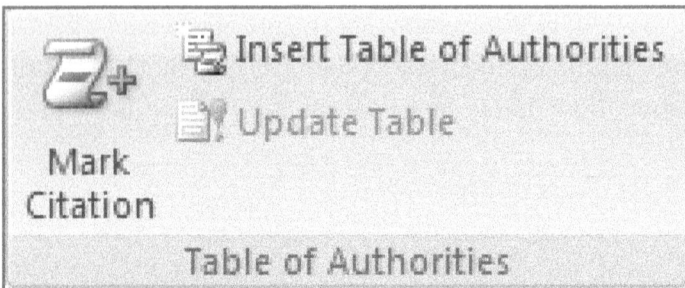

Figure 123: Table of Authorities

206

Table of Authorities Group

Under this tab group, you can insert a table of authorities into your document. First, you will have to mark citations, and then insert them as your table of authorities. You can also update an existing table of authorities, in case you have one already, and you have made some changes to it.

To insert a table of authorities into your document, first mark your citations. When you are done marking your citations, click on the "**Insert Table of Authorities**," command button as shown above. Bear in mind that when a button is inactive, it means you cannot use it right now. You can only update the existing tables in your document.

CHAPTER 5: MAILING TAB

~~**~~

Introduction

Welcome to the fifth chapter. I hope you are learning many things, right? Under this fifth chapter, we will discuss more about mailings. Here, you can Create, Start Mail Merge, Write & Insert Fields, Review Results, and Finish your mailing work. All these activities are called tab groups, and we will discuss them as such. Did you know you could send email messages, using the Outlook program in Microsoft Office Suite?

Figure 124: Create group

Create Group

Under the Create tab group, you can create envelopes and labels to use in your mailings. Mailings is all about sending and receiving email messages, using the Microsoft email services. Most of these services need an internet connection, so that they can work well. You may not really need to use them, anyway. However, in case you need them, here is how to use them. Remember, computing is like playing a game. Things change at any time, and you will have to be up to date to learn new things in technology.

To create an envelope, click on the "**Envelopes**," command button as shown above, and follow the on-screen instructions, that will show up. As mentioned earlier, you may need an internet connection for these features to work. You may be asked to pay for the service as well. You will need to type the delivery address and then add it to the document, or print it out. Using the "**Labels**," command button can also make you able to enter envelopes as well. For these features to work, make sure the Microsoft Outlook mail client is the default mail client on your computer.

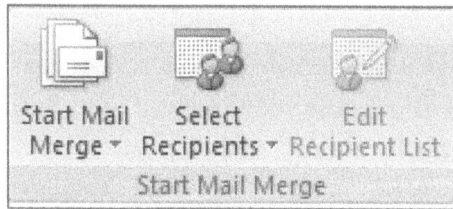

Start Mail Merge Group

Under this tab group, you can be able to start the Mail Merge, Select Recipients, and Edit your Recipient List, if you have some. To use a Mail Merge feature, you can use letters, e-mail messages, envelopes, labels, normal Word Document, or you can use a step-by-step Mail Merge Wizard.

To use a Mail Merge feature, click on the "**Start Mail Merge**," command button as shown above, and a drop down menu will open. In that menu, you can merge mails using letters, e-mail messages, envelopes, labels, normal Word Document, or a step-by-step Mail Merge Wizard program, to help you do the required actions in this area.

To select your recipients to send messages to, click on the "**Select Recipients**," command button as shown in the picture above. There, you can type a new list, use your existing list, or select recipients from your Outlook email contacts. For now, you cannot be able to edit your recipient list, because you do not have one, and that is why the command button appears dimmed.

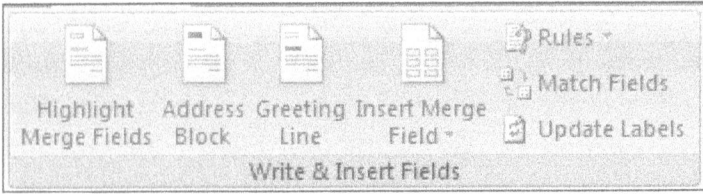

Write & Insert Fields Group

Under this tab group, you can be able to Highlight Merge Fields, use the Address Block, use the Greeting Line, Insert Merge Field, view Rules, Match Fields, and Update your existing levels. Remember, in order to perform any computing action, a command button must be active.

As shown in the picture above, none of the command icons is active. Why? Because we do not have anything to do with them right now. You can only highlight merge fields when you have them. You cannot be able to use the greeting line when you have no e-mail connection setup. This means we cannot be able to write or insert any fields into our e-mail message until we fix the problem of configuring our Outlook e-mail client on our computer. Check the "**Create**," tab group above to create this, and you will see all these commands becoming active.

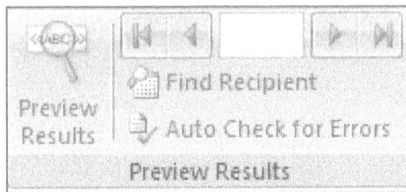

Figure 127: Preview results

Preview Results Group

Under this tab group, you can be able to preview your results for setting up your e-mail client. You can find your recipients or check for errors in your settings, automatically. You may not be able to

210

use this tab group and others after it until you created your envelopes and labels as discussed earlier. As you can see above, none of the command buttons is active. Why? Because you do not need these command buttons at this time. Only active commands can work when clicked. If you see commands appearing inactive, then there is a reason behind this.

To preview your results, click on the **"Preview Results,"** command button as shown above. To find your listed recipients or contacts another word, use the **"Find Recipient,"** command button as shown above. However, make sure you have these buttons in their active mode, or else you can click and nothing will happen. To automatically check for errors in your e-mail client settings, click the **"Auto Check for Errors,"** command button.

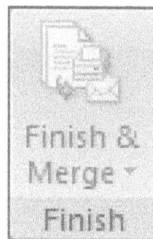

Figure 128: Finish group

Finish Group

This tab group is for finishing your e-mail client setup. Nevertheless, you have to check for errors before you finish the setup for your e-mail client. As you may recall, if the buttons are inactive, it means the commands are not needed right now. Use the **"Finish and Merge,"** command button to finish and merge your e-mail client settings. This is the last command button in the **Mailings Tab**. You can see that, if you have not created any envelope or levels in the first tab group, you cannot be able to do any other commands following it. The most important tab group here is the **Create** tab. Make sure you setup everything correctly in this section before you continue. Thanks for reading up to this far.

You still have three more chapters ahead of you to finish reading. At the end of chapter 8 of this book (**Part VII**), you will read more about how to write your academic papers, using the Microsoft Word 2007 program. Most scholars use this program to write their research papers, reports and many other great documents. Bear in mind that we are discussing the mail features of this program, some of which you may not necessary need to use. Pick what you can use and run with it.

CHAPTER 6: REVIEW TAB

~~**~~

Introduction

Welcome to the sixth chapter of this simplified guide to Microsoft Word program. Thank you very much for reading from the first chapter this chapter. Now, you will learn about Proofing, Comments, Tracking, Changes, Compare and Protect. These are also known as tab groups, and they may look almost the same in all Office programs.

Figure 129: Proofing group

Proofing Group

Under this tab group, you will learn how to use the Spelling & Grammar in Microsoft Word program. You will learn how to research and how to use a thesaurus feature, which will help you use better words for your document. You will surely need these features when writing your academic papers. You will also learn how to use the translation feature. Did you know you could translate your document into many different languages, even if you do not know the languages, yourself? You will learn how to use the word count feature also. You will also learn to use the Translation ScreenTip feature, and even set the language for use in your Word Program.

To correct your writings, click on the "**Spelling & Grammar,**" command button as shown above, and a spell check feature will open. Bear in mind that the checking of your document will begin from the first error in your document, which can be from the first page or anywhere else. This means the cursor will move to the place where the correction is needed in your document being in the first or last page.

To search for words and their meaning in your document, or on a website, use the "Research," command button as shown in the picture above. Here, a task pane will open to the right hand side of your window. You can then type the word you want to learn more about, and then click on the arrow next to the search field, and the results will appear below the search field. Make sure you are connected to the Internet before you begin the searching.

To use a thesaurus, click on the "**Thesaurus**," command button as shown above, and a task pane will appear on the far right hand side of your document. Here, you can enter a word into the search field, and click the **GO** button represented by an arrow. Here, dictionary definitions will appear. Note that if you choose "**All reference Books**," your word will not be defined for you until you are connected to the Internet. Use Thesaurus: English United Kingdom, or Thesaurus: English United States," to get your word defined offline. These thesauruses must be downloaded to your computer before they can be used effectively.

To translate words or your document, you need to be connected to the Internet, and then click on the "**Translate**," command button as shown above. This will also open a task pane where you have to enter the word you want to translate, and choose the language and hit the **GO** button. You can also setup the translation screen tip by selecting a language in the list. To do this, click on the "**Translation ScreenTip**," command button as shown in the picture above, and select the language from the list that will appear. The screen tip is always turned off by default.

Use the "**Set Language**," command button to change the default language for your Microsoft Word Program. Use the "**Word Count**," command button to see how many words you have in your document so far. You will need to know the number of words when writing academic papers. This will allow you to see how many pages is your current document.

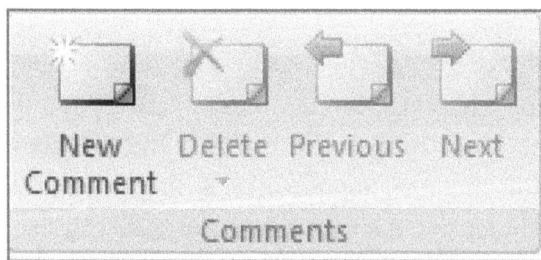

Figure 130: Comments group

Comments Group

Under comments tab group, you can insert a new comment into your document. Do you mark someone's work electronically? Then you will have to use this feature to do this. You can delete the comments, go to previous, or next comments in your document.

To insert a new comment into your document, hit the "**New Comment**," command button as shown in the picture above, and a comment placeholder will appear in your document. You will need to type in your comments to your student, and save the document. This feature is also great for book editors before they produce final copies of their edits. The author has to check the comments and agree or disagree with the commentator, an editor's comments.

To delete an existing comment, click on the "**Delete**," command button as shown above. If you do not have any comments inserted in your document, you will not be able to delete anything. You will not be able to move to the previous or to the next comment. This means these command buttons will not be active as well.

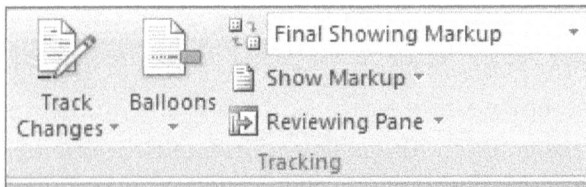

Figure 131: Tracking Group

Tracking Group

Under this tab group, you will learn about Track Changes, Balloons, Final Showing Markup, Show Markup, and the Reviewing Pane. To see these commands, click on the "**Review Tab**," and then look for the tracking tab group in the middle-top of the document. Under the tracking tab group, you can use the "**Track Changes**," command button to change the tracking. This will help you track all changes to your document, including the insertion, deletion and formatting changes, made to your document.

To change your tracking options or your username, click on the small arrow on the "**Track Changes**," command button as shown above. To setup how to show revisions, click on the "**Balloons**," command button as shown above. From here, you can show revisions in balloons, or show all revisions inline. The show only comments and formatting in balloons is the default setting. The markups to show by defaults are comments, ink, insertions and deletions, formatting, markup area highlight and reviewers, but you can remove some of these by deselecting them. You can set the review pane to horizontal or to vertical. You can also select the final showing markup, final, original showing markup or the original options. These are displays for review options.

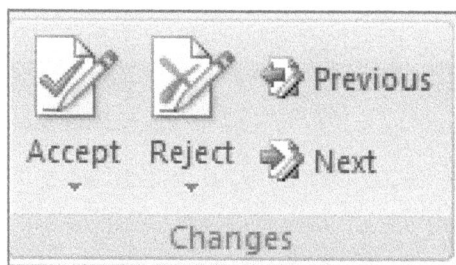

Figure 132: Changes Group

Changes Group

Under the changes tab group, you can either reject or accept the changes suggested. Imagine, you wrote a book and someone else edited it adding his/her comments, using this comment feature. The person will send you the work and you have to agree or accept his/her comments to be applied into your document, or you can reject them. You can also move to the previous or to the next comments to accept or reject comments.

To accept someone's comments and apply them into your document, click on the "**Accept**," button as shown above. You can also use the little arrow in the 'accept' command in order to choose what to accept. You can accept and move to the next comment, accept the change, accept all changes shown, or accept all the changes in your document at once. You can repeat these actions for rejecting. This means you can reject and move to the next comment if you hit on the small arrow near the "**Reject**," command button as shown above. You can also use the "**Previous**," and the "**Next**," command buttons as shown in the picture above to move back and forth in your document.

217

Figure 133: Compare

Compare Group

Under the compare tab group, you can compare different documents from the same author or from different authors. If different people revised your document, you just need to use this tool to compare the differences and then decide which one is the best. You can also show the source documents from this tab group.

To compare the two documents, click on the "**Compare**," command button as shown above. Here, you can compare two versions of a document, or combine revisions from multiple authors into a single document. Thinking about manually merging the revisions from your different reviewers, how difficult will this be? However, if you use this feature in Microsoft Word program, you will do this work in a very easy way. You can be able to show the source document, if you like after combining different versions.

Figure 134: Protect

Protect Group

Under this tab group, you can be able to protect your document. The formatting and editing of your document can be restricted here, and you can do it yourself for security reasons. You will have to sign up for the protection service from Microsoft online services. The default settings for any document are unrestricted, but you can protect your document from this tab, if you want. Here, you can protect your document. You can restrict the formatting and the editing of your work, but you must set this up using your Windows Live ID/Microsoft Account. You can also manage your credentials from here.

To do all these activities, you must set them up, using your Microsoft Account. You may not really need to use the Information Rights Management, because you will have to pay at the end of your trial service. Do you really want to protect your documents, including your files and folders? Then consider using the "**Protected Folder**," from IObit. Go to www.iobit.com to get the trial. You will also have to register the software after sometime.

CHAPTER 7: VIEW TAB

~~**~~

Introduction

Welcome to the seventh chapter. Under this tab, you will learn about Document Views, Show/Hide feature, Zoom, Window and Macros. Changing a view of your document makes you worry sometimes, especially if you do not know what to do. The document views are very important for you. Read below to discover many great features of your MS Word program.

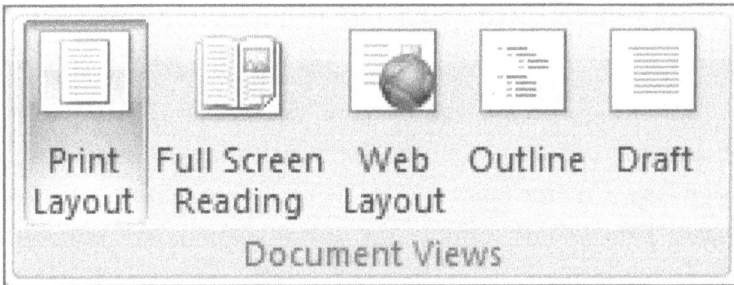

Figure 135: Document View

Document Views Group

Under this tab group, you will learn about document views such as, Print Layout, Full Screen Reading, Outline, Web Layout and Draft views. You will have to understand these document views to stay out of trouble. Sometimes when you change a view without your knowledge, you will first panic before you fix the problem. The Print Layout is the default document view. This view makes your document look like the way it will look when printed. You can also find the command button for this view and other views on the status bar of your MS Word. For more information about the bars and other important tabs, please read chapter 8 of this book.

To switch to the full screen reading that will make your document look like an open booklet, click on the "**Full Screen Reading**," command button as shown in the picture above. The web layout document view will make your document look like a webpage. The outline view will make your document look funny. Use the draft view to see some hidden formatting in your document. This view is great for those who are formatting documents for publication such as e-book formats. Do you know you can write a book in MS Word and convert it to a Kindle readable book?

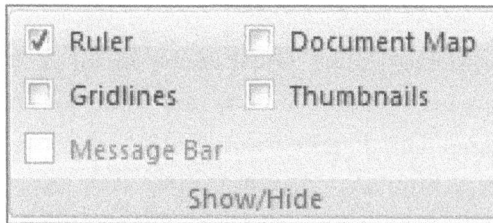

Figure 136: Show/Hide

Show/Hide Group

Under the show/hide tab group, you can hide or show some items and features in your document. You can show or hide your Document Map, Gridlines, Thumbnails, Message Bar, and Rulers. Do you know you have rulers in your document? You can use these rulers to measure your pages, if you want

To show/hide any of these items and features in your document, click on a checkbox next to the feature that you want to show or hide, and it will be shown or hidden. You can hide rulers in your document by un-checking the checkbox next to the ruler. You can show gridlines in your document, if you want. These lines will not be shown when you print the document.

To show thumbnails, click on the checkbox next to the thumbnails as shown in the picture above. The document map shows bookmarks or headings in your document. Thumbnails show the pages in your document on the left hand side of your document as thumbnail pictures.

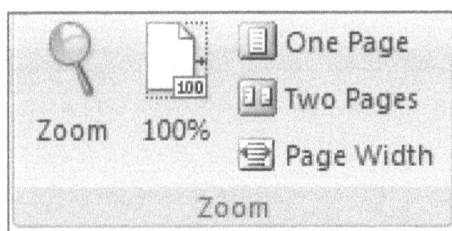

Figure 137: Zoom

Zoom Group

Under the zoom tab group, you can zoom in or zoom out your work. This increases the size of your text while the text's actual size remains the same. The default zoom is 100%, but you can change it to any zooming number. You can view you page as one page, which is the default view, or as two pages. You can setup the page width of your document from this tab group.

To see more zooming options, click on the "**Zoom,**" command button as shown in the picture above. You can set everything from there. Everything such as page width, text width, and whole document can be found from here. Now, select your desired settings and enjoy the look of your document.

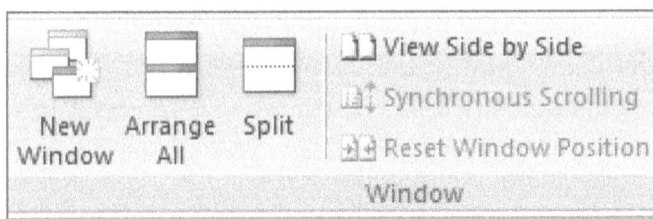

Figure 138: Window

Window Group

Under this tab group, you can show the same document in a new window. You can arrange all or split the document into different viewpoints. You can split the document when you want to work on different parts at the same time. If you want to keep your eyes on the table of contents, while you work in other parts of document, you can split the document into two parts.

To view your document on different windows, click on the "**New Window**," command button. The new window view will have a different title altogether. To arrange all, click on the "**Arrange All**," command button as shown in the picture above. To split the document into two parts, click on the "**Split**," command button as shown above. You can also view your documents side by side, if they are all open at the same time. You can use the synchronous scrolling or reset Window position. However, for now, these commands are inactive because there are no two open windows. You can also switch from a window to a window, if you have two open windows at the same time.

Figure 139: Macros

Macros Group

Macros are features that are not enabled by default. They can help you run some commands, automatically. You can either view macros or record macros by clicking the small arrow near the macros command button as shown below.

To record macros, hit the "**Macros**," command button as shown above. To select whether to record or view macros, click on the small arrow near the macros command button as shown above. Please be careful with macros because they can be linked to a button or to the keyboard. You can create or deleting existing macros, if you want to do so. You can stop, or pause macros' recording process by clicking on the right buttons when the recording is taking place. If a document is having macros running, you have to take care before you open them. Your antivirus program or the security features of your computer may stop macros from running for security reasons. Why? Because in this way, macros can run viruses and other malicious programs.

CHAPTER 8: HIDDEN TABS

~~**~~

Introduction

Welcome to chapter 8. This chapter discusses other hidden tabs that you cannot see until they are needed. These tabs show up in the menu bar when you need them. They also come with their own tab groups and command buttons just like other tabs we discussed so fat in this book. In this chapter, I will also share with you some important features of Microsoft Word 2007 program. These features include bars, menus, buttons, and other important commands. After learning all these, we will have a look at how to write academic papers, using different formats.

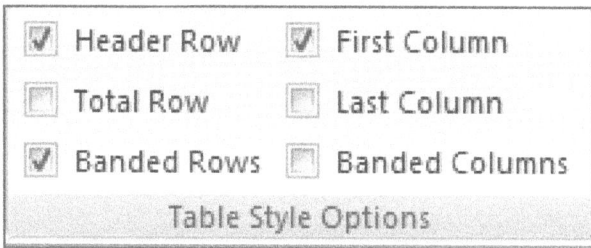

Figure 140: Table Style Options

Design Tab

This tab with its own tab groups appear when you inserted a table into your document. You will have the table style options, tab group, table styles and draw borders (tab groups under this). Under the table style options, you can choose to show things like, Header Row, Total Row, and Banded Rows. You can also decide to show things like, First Column, Last Column, and Banded Columns. All of these commands are found under the Design Tab.

Figure 141: Styles

There are many table styles to choose from. You can also use shadings and borders when formatting your tables. You can draw a table or erase existing cells, using the eraser. To see a live preview of a table style, click on it. To apply shadings or borders, click on the shading or borders command buttons as shown in the picture above.

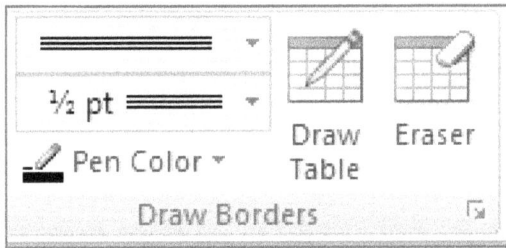

Figure 142: Draw Borders

Under the draw borders tab group, you can draw tables, using the "**Draw Table**," command button as shown above. You can also erase the existing tables or cells, using the "**Eraser**," command button. You can choose the drawing styles and the pen colour as shown in the picture above.

Layout Tab

The layout tab is also found when you insert a table into your document. This tab has its own tab groups such as, table, rows & columns, merge, cell size, alignment and data. These tab groups contain their own commands buttons and icons in the ribbon, just like any other tab discussed earlier.

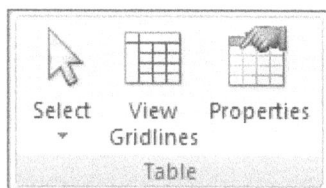

Figure 143: Table

Under the table tab group, you can select a cell, column, row, or even the whole table. You may also decide to show gridlines in the document. You can also show properties of a table from that tab. Use the "**Select**," command button as shown in the picture above, to select parts of the table such as cells, or the whole table.

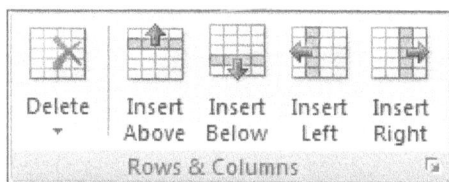

Figure 144: Rows and Columns

Under rows & columns tab group, you can delete rows, columns, cells or the whole table, using the small arrow next to the "**Delete**," command button that will appear. You can also insert rows or columns on top, to the left, right or to the bottom of any existing rows or columns.

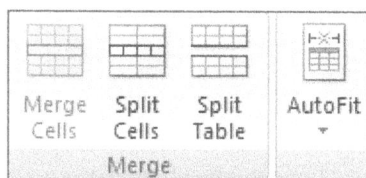

Figure 145: Merge

Under the merge tab group, you can merge cells, split cells, or split a table. All these features will only appear when you select a table, and then click on the "**Layout Tab**," in the menu bar.

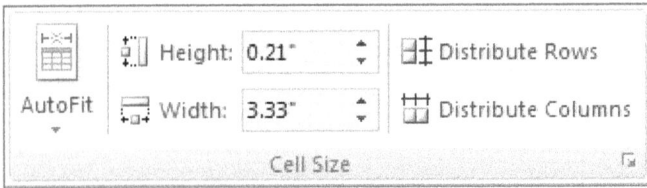

Figure 146: Cell Size

Under cell size tab group, you can see the AutoFit command button. You can auto fit contents, windows and column width. You can also set the height and width of a column, using the small arrows or by typing the number into the fields. The default column height is 0.21 pt, and its width is 3.33 pt. you can also distribute rows and columns equally.

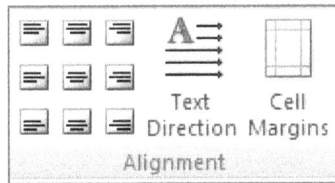

Figure 147: Alignment

Under the alignment tab group, you can align text in cells to the top-right, middle-right, bottom-right, centre-right, top-centre, bottom-centre, top-left, centre-left and bottom-left of the cells. You can also setup the text direction and cell margins under this tab group, using command buttons as shown above.

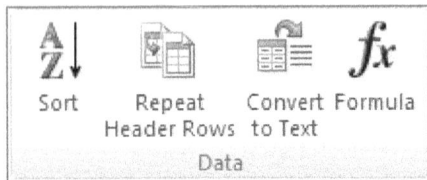

Figure 148: Data

Under data tab group, you can sort your data alphabetically or numerically. Just select your data and then click on the "**Sort**," command button as shown in the picture above. You can also repeat header rows or convert an existing table into a text data. You

228

can even use formulas to execute some important commands in a simple way. You will have to work with formulas a lot more in the MS Excel Program.

Format Tab

The **Format Tab** appears whenever you selected a picture or a text box in your document. If you select a picture in your document, you will see a format tab added to the menu bar on top of your document. Here, you can see other tab groups that you can use to adjust and format your picture the way you like. The first tab group from the left to right is "**Adjust**," and you can use it to adjust your currently selected picture.

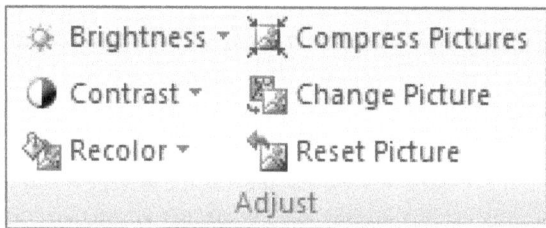

Figure 149: Adjust

Adjust Group

Here, you can adjust your currently selected picture. You can adjust the brightness, contrast, recolor, and reset the picture, if you want. You can compress pictures in the whole document, or change this currently selected picture with a different picture from your document.

To adjust the brightness of the currently selected picture, click on the "**Brightness**," command button as shown in the picture above. There are many things or options to choose from. To apply some contrast to the current picture, click on the "**Contrast**," command button as shown above. You can compress your inserted pictures so that their size is slightly smaller than the actual sizes. This is great if you want to upload or send your document over e-mail. It will make your document lighter than it actually is. This option is also good to save your disk space. If you made some changes to the picture and you are not happy with that, hit the "**Reset Picture**," command button as shown above, and the picture will return to its original formatting.

Figure 150: Picture Styles Group

Picture Styles Group—there are many picture styles to choose from. For this reason, we are not going to take our time going through each style. To see them, just hit on the picture in your document, and you will see them in the middle-top of your window. Here, you can change the picture shapes, picture border and picture effects.

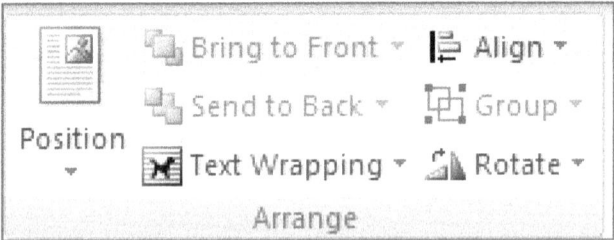

Figure 151: Arrange

Arrange Group

Under the arrange tab group, you can position the picture, send it to back or bring it to front. This arrangement works well when working with pictures wrapped with text or other objects, and you want to see the picture behind or in front of the other objects.

To position the currently selected picture, hit "**Position**," command button as shown in the picture above. You can also hit on the small arrow below the position button, and the same action is executed. Here, you will see many different ways to position your picture in the document. To use the text wrapping options, click on the "**Text Wrapping**," command button as shown in the picture above, and choose from the drop down menu that will appear. You can also use the "**Align**," command to align the picture in your document. You can use the "**Rotate**," command to rotate the currently selected picture.

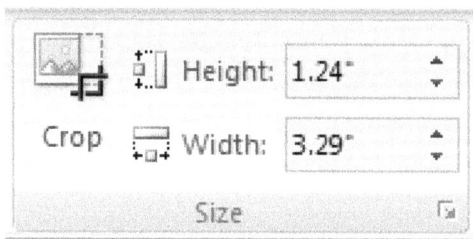

Figure 152: Size tab Group

Size Group

Under the size tab group, you can setup the size of your selected picture. You can set the height and widths. You can even crop the picture, if you wish. Use the upper arrows to increase the size of the width, or height of a picture, and use the lower arrow to decrease them. You can even enter a number into the text field next to the width or height, to increase or decrease its size. To crop the selected picture, hit on the "**Crop**," command button, and some borders will appear on the picture. Adjust the borders, and the parts you do not want will be removed.

Other Tabs

As we mentioned earlier, you may see different tabs appearing, depending on what you are doing with your MS Word program. The format tab can also appear, if you inserted a textbook or WordArt into your document. When you inert a text box into your document, you will have the "**Format**," tab appearing in the menu bar. This format tab contains other tab groups, just like any other tab discussed earlier in this book. The tabs groups in this tab can be, text, text box styles, shadow effects, 3D effects, arrange and size. Under the "**Text**," tab group, you can draw a text box, change the text direction, create link or break any existing links. Under the textbox, styles tab group, you can choose from many textbox styles available. You can also change the shape field, shape outline or change this current shape type. You can do many changes for the shadow effects, depending on how you want the shadows to appear. You can even apply different 3D effects to your textbox. The positioning for the textbox is more like that of a picture discussed above. You can also set the size of a textbox field, using the "**Size**," tab group to the far right of the window.

Other Features

We must talk in MS Word Program about many other important features. These features include, menus, bars, and other important buttons that you really need to know about. What comes to your mind when I say, click on the "Home Tab" in the menu bar? Well, to know what I want you to do; you have to know what the "Menu bar" is and where to find it.

Figure 153: Office Button

Office Button—Office button is a button found on the top-left corner of Microsoft Word Program window in MS Word 2007. This button is replaced by the "**File**," button in MS Word 2010 and in the earlier versions of Office products. This is how the Office button looks like in MS Word 2007 program. You can click on that button to do many things with your current document. Click on this button to open, save, create a new document, save as, or to access other MS Word Options. You can use this button to even print this current document. You can use this button to open a document saved somewhere on your document.

Figure 154: Quick Access Toolbar

Quick Access Toolbar—this is a bar found on the top-right of the Office Button. You can use this bar to add commands to the top of your program, so that when you need them, you get them quickly. You can add or remove command buttons from this bar, if you wish. On my Quick Access Toolbar, you can see I have added three command buttons that I like to use most. The command buttons are **Save**, **Undo** and **Redo**. The undo button is located on the right side of the Office Button, and the Redo or repeat button is located after the small arrow. The small arrow between the redo and undo buttons is to choose what to undo, in case I have made many changes in my document. It will disappear if it is not needed. The other little arrow next to the redo button is to add more commands to the Quick Access Toolbar. To add more commands, click on that arrow and a list of commands will appear. Clicking on any of those commands in the list adds their command buttons.

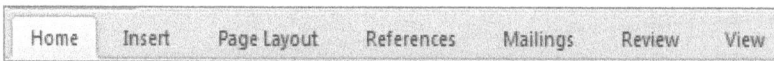

Figure 155: Menu Bar

Menu Bar—this is a bar that contains tabs and Help Button to the far right hand side of the window. The tabs are seven in number from right to left, with the exception of the hidden tabs as discussed. Use the "**Menu Bar**," to do more with your document. You can learn more about tabs and their tab groups from chapter 1 through chapter 8 of this book. There are tab groups with many command buttons under each. You need tabs to do many different things with your document. This menu bar also contains the Office Button to the far left.

Figure 156: Status Bar

Status Bar—this is a bar below the MS Word program window. It lies on top of the Taskbar of your Windows Operating System. On this bar, you can view page numbers of your document on the far bottom-left. You can also view word count in your document, which is good for your academic writing tips discussed below. On this bar, you can also see if your document is busy or not. The book and pen icons show if someone is busy typing or not. When you type, you will see the pen writing. You can also see your current typing language on this bar. You can see the view options and the zoom tools on the far right of this bar.

Figure 157: Title bar

Title Bar—this bar is located opposite to the Status Bar discussed above. It is located on the top part of the MS Word Program window. It contains the title or the name of your current document to the middle, command buttons (Minimize, Maximize/Restore and Close buttons) to the far right. It also contains the Quick Access Toolbar to the far left corner.

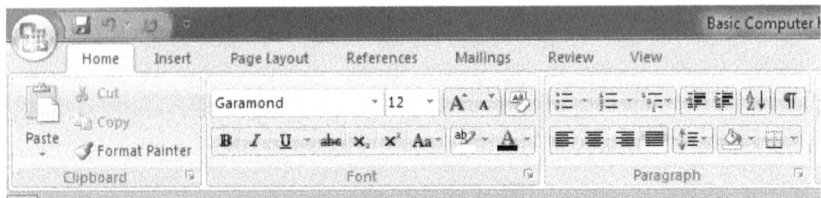

Figure 158: Office Word Ribbon

Ribbon—this is the area under the tabs. It contains all command buttons, which changes whenever you are on a certain tab. These command buttons are grouped under tab groups as discussed earlier in this book from chapter 1 to chapter 8. All the command

234

buttons for text alignment in the Home Tab are located on the Ribbon.

Figure 159: Control buttons

Control Buttons—these are three buttons located to the top-right of any open window. They are also known as control buttons. You can use them to minimize, maximize/restore, or close the MS Word program window. A button that looks like a dash in the picture above is the "**Minimize button,**" and you can use it to minimize the MS Word program window as mentioned above. The other button in the middle is used to restore or maximize a window. You can find these buttons on all open windows, especially when using other OS apart from Windows 8.0. You can use the (X) button to close a document. Please make sure you save your work before you click this!

Figure 160: Word Help Button

Help Button—this is a button found on the Menu Bar. It is used to learn more about MS Word program. If you really want to read more about Microsoft Word, click on this button. The button can be used to search for help both online and offline. You can learn many things about Word 2007 program from the Help and Support, using this Help button.

Figure 161: Zoom slider

Zooming—this is the area on the Status Bar as discussed earlier. Use this to increase the size of your work, especially when you do not want to change the font size in your document. I use this when

I want to edit or proofread a book. Clicking on the (-) or the (+) buttons will increase or decrease the size of your document (text). The default size for your document is 100% as shown in the picture above.

Scroll Bar—this is a bar that appears on the right hand side of your document. You use this bar to scroll through your document. The bar can also appear below the document working area, if your document is too wide, and it cannot fit into the work area. The bar can appear below the work area, if you zoom in your work to 160% because this can make your document larger than normal.

If you like learning these features, don't hesitate to share your thoughts with me. Let's talk at maluthabiel@gmail.com

CHAPTER 9: ACADEMIC WRITING TIPS

~~**~~

When you write your assignments, you are told to format your work according to the academic requirements. What are these academic requirements? This section of the book is dedicated to helping you identify the most command academic writing formatting errors. The common academic paper elements include word count, page numbering, text alignment, font face, font size, and font colour.

What does it means when your teacher says, "Use Arial, size 12"? This means to set your writing type to Arial font face, and your text size is 12. However, how do you know where to find the "Arial," font face? You can surely look at chapter 1 for more details on formatting using the "**Home Tab**," in MS Word.

Text Alignment

Most universities recommend the "**Justified**," text alignment formatting. This text formatting makes your text to appear equal on all margins on both right and left sides. This book is formatted with the "**Justified**," text alignment. To align your text as justified, make sure you are on the "**Home Tab**," then click this button in the Paragraph Group. In addition, you must select the whole text or paragraph that you want to format. For more information about text alignment, kindly check the first chapter of this book.

Fonts Formatting

Font formatting includes font face, font colour, and font size. Most universities recommend using the Arial font face or Times New Roman. Font face is simply a writing type or style. Font face makes your text look different depending on the font face you have chosen. The good thing is that you can preview any font face before you apply it to your document.

To apply a font face to your text, select the text and click on this button [Calibri (Body) ▾] (small arrow) to choose your font face from the list that will appear. To change a font face, just point to the font face that you would like to apply to your text before you click on it so that you see a live preview of that font face. If you like it, click on it to apply it to your selected text. The default font face in MS Word program is "**Calibri (Body),**" but you can change it to any font face available.

Font Colour—most universities do not support any colour apart from the black or automatic colour. In academic writing, you will lose marks if you format your text with any different colours apart from the automatic colour. To avoid any other colours in your text, select the whole document, and then use the automatic colour to apply this colour to the whole document at once.

To apply a certain colour to some text in your document, select the text and then click on the colour button [A ▾] to apply the current colour to the selected text. The default colour in Word is "**Red,**" but you can change to any colour of your choice by clicking on the small arrow near the colour's command button as shown in the above picture. Clicking on the arrow will allow you to see a list of available colours.

Font Size—most universities recommend size 12 or 14, depending on the type of the paper you are writing. Most people support size 12 for research assignments. To apply font size to your text, select your document and then click on the "**Grow Font,**" icon [A˄] to move from size 11 to size 12 at once. The default font size in MS Word is size 11. You can do font formatting under the "**Home Tab,**" in MS Word program. Other Office applications also share the same features with MS Word as mentioned earlier in this book. Mastering the MS Word program will help you master other programs as well. You can set the font highlight colour, but not for your academic paper please.

Line Spacing

You may use 1.5 or 2.0 line spacing, depending on the requirements of your university, and the type of paper you are writing. To apply the line spacing format, select the whole text, and

then click on the "**Line Spacing**," button and choose the line spacing numbering from the list that will appear. You can add the space before or after a paragraph from there, if you want. If you add spaces before and after paragraphs, this will make your writing much easier. It will create paragraphs as you press the enter key on your keyboard. However, this is only good in block paragraphing.

Page Numbering

Page numbering is very important in academic writing. Sometimes, you want to begin page numbering from the first point of your main points in your assignment. How can you do this? This is important especially when you have to save your assignment as one document. Sometimes, you may save your cover page or table of contents page as different documents. What if you are told to save your assignment as one document? There are many ways to insert page numbers into your assignment.

Most universities recommend placing your page numbers on the bottom-centre of your document. To do this, click on the **Insert Tab**, and then look for **Page Number** in the **Header & Footer** tab group. Click on the page number command button, and then point to Bottom of Page format and a submenu will open. On the submenu that will appear, click on the "**Plain Number 2**," format to choose bottom-centre. It all depends on the requirements of your university. Please ask your assistant, professor, or instructor.

Page Count

Page count depends on the nature of your assignment. Your university may require certain page numbering for assignments. To reduce page numbers, please edit your work and remove any unnecessary text that is making your page count to exceed what is required by your university. A 1,500-word count assignment ranges from 10-15 typed pages, depending on your font size, font face, and line spacing.

Word Count

Word count is to determine how many words per assignment. It is one of the requirements of most universities today. Nevertheless, how do you know how many words you have in your assignment? You can determine this by selecting the whole of your assignment text and then look on the bottom-left corner of your screen.

You can also select parts of your assignment to determine the word count number. Each section of your assignment may consist of a certain number of words. If your assignment consists of 1,500 words, and it has three main questions or sections, make sure each section is exactly 500 words or slightly above that. If you exceed to 10% above the required word count, they may not grade assignment, or you will lose marks for that.

Source Acknowledgement

When you write an assignment, you must use sources. The sources can be in a written or in an audio format. They can be front printed or electronic materials such as print books, e-books, or web pages. There are many ways to reference your sources. You can also check the fourth chapter of this book for more information about how to use MS Word program.

APA—this is Abbreviation of Personal Allowance or American Psychological Association. There are fifth and sixth editions of this reference style, and you can use MS Word to learn how this style looks like. The fifth edition of APA style of a single reference entry looks like the one below.

Monyjok, J. (2013). *Microsoft Word in Academic Writing*. **Juba:** Discipleship Press.

There are many ways to reference your sources. Some universities such as South African Theological Seminary use the in-text citation and Harvard style of reference. Ask your tutor to tell you what style of reference your university supports before you use any style. The in-text citation refers to quoting and citing your sources in the text. For example, "For God so loved the world that he gave his only begotten Son" (John 3:16). I have quoted and cited the text in this example. Another example is, "South Sudan needs a transformation process that is both spiritual and physical," (Monyjok 2014:12). This citation includes the author name (Monyjok), year of publication (2014), and the page number where the quotation was taken (12).

Assignment Properties

Your assignment must include an introduction, body and a conclusion. Before these parts, you need a cover page, table of contents and a bibliography. The design of your assignment's cover page will defer from school to another. The requirement is that you have to align the text to the centre of the cover page (for some schools).

Cover Page—this is a 1-page document. Your cover page can contain the name of your school as the first item entered. The faculty or department that you are studying in can follow the school name. The assignment title and number can follow the department or faculty name, then your name comes in. Under your name, you can enter the name of your teacher, tutor or professor, and then the assignment due date.

Table of Contents Page—this is a 1-page document. Here, you can list your main points in the assignment, including your introduction and conclusion. Make sure that your points appear in this page as they will appear in your assignment. You will have to use the headings formatting styles to avoid page numbering errors. Remember to use automatic colouring when saving your final assignment.

Body Pages—here the page count depends on the nature of your assignment. You will discuss your points from the first to the last, as your points appear in your table of contents page. Make sure your points appear in a logical order. This is how people write books and learning these steps and principles, will help you pass well, if you put them into practice as you write your academic papers. You have to start discussing your points from the introduction to the conclusion pages.

Reference Page—this is another 1-page document. Nevertheless, you may need to include all in a single document. To avoid any page numbering formatting errors, make sure you begin your page numbering from the introduction page to the conclusion page. You have to write your cover page, table of contents page and the bibliography pages before the introduction page, so that they are not numbered. You do not need to number your cover page or table of contents page. However, if your assignment must be printed before marking, then put the bibliography at the last page even though your page numbers will appear on it. The cover and the table of contents pages will not be numbered. However, how can you jump over these two pages in your document? It is very simple to jump over any pages at the beginning of your document.

To jump some pages in your document without numbering them, click on the beginning of the first line in the page where you want to begin page numbering. For example, if you want your page numbering to start on the introduction page. Now, click on the **"Page Layout Tab,"** and look for **"Breaks,"** in **Page Setup** tab group. Click on the **"Breaks,"** command button and then select the **"Next Page,"** command under the **Section Break** group. Now, click on the **"Insert Tab,"** and then click on page number command button. You will have to remove any page numbering first. After removing page numbers, click the format page numbers and select the start at, and then click **OK** to save the changes. Now, click on the **Footer** command in the **Header & Footer** tab group. Here, you will have to remove any footer in your document. Then click on the edit footer command. Now, click on the link to previous command and close the **Header & Header**. Click on the **Insert Tab** again and then select **Footer**. Now, choose from the available footer designs, and then close the **Header & Footer** window again. Now, your page numbering begins from where you want, up to the end of the document.

Assignment Cover Sheet

Emmanuel Christian College

Department of Theology

Homiletics Assignment 1

By

John Monyjok Maluth

Tutor: Rev. Andrew Bashir

May 16th 2014

Figure 162: Assignment Cover

Cover Page Template

Different schools and universities use different designs for the cover page. Yet, most use this design. You have to ask your school about cover designs. If your school has a format to use, use it so that you will not lose marks. You can lose points if you do not follow your school's design requirements. The cover page must contain the following information: school name, department, course, assignment, a student name, tutor's name, and submission dates for the assignment.

Table of Contents

Contents

Introduction 1

What is Homiletics? 2

Biblical Homiletics 3

Secular Homiletics 4

How to use Homiletics 5

Homiletics Examples 6

Conclusion 7

Bibliography 8

Figure 163: Table of Contents

Table of Contents Template

Your table of contents contains the main points in your assignment or book. Wring an assignment paper is like writing a book, but of a different kind of course. This is why if you master academic writing, you are likely to be a good writer. The body of your assignment begins with page 1 in your document. It must begin with the first item in the table of contents. In this example, it begins with the introduction to your assignment as a whole. You can title this page as **Table of Contents**, or just **Contents** as I did in the example above. Align the title of your page to the centre of the document and make it bold.

Bibliography Page

Bibliography

Monyjok, J. (2012). *Biblical Homiletics*. Juba, South Sudan: Discipleship Press.

Moses, M. (1988). *Homiletics Principles*. Chicago, USA: CBA Press.

Nura, K. (1999). *Using Homiletics*. Juba, South Sudan: Discipleship Press.

Omot, S. (2013). *Secular Homiletics*. Yei, South Sudan: Discipleship Press.

Peter, K. (2014). *Public Speaking Tips*. Malakal, South Sudan: Juba Press.

Figure 164: Bibliography

Bibliography Template

This sample bibliography page was designed using APA Referencing Style 6th Edition. Here, you begin with the author's surname, followed by a comma. Then you insert the first letter of his/her first name (initial) followed by a period (.) or full stop. Now, you insert the date of publication of that book in brackets, followed by a period or full stop. Now, insert the title of the book or article (*Italicized*), the full stop or period follows. Now, you can insert a city or town of publication, followed by a publisher's name.

The word, *Biblio* is a Greek word that means "**Book**," in English. Bibliography therefore is a graph or list of books used in your work. When you write any academic paper, you must use some sources. At the end of your work, you have to acknowledge those sources, and this is the bibliography or list of books used. Your bibliography can be **Works Cited**, depending on how you used your sources in the assignment. It can also be titled as **Works Consulted**, in case you never quoted or cited any of these sources after reading them. For sure, there are many styles to utilize.

For more information about writing academic papers, please contact me today at maluthabiel@gmail.com

BOOK 6: MICROSOFT POWERPOINT 2007

INTRODUCTION TO MICROSOFT POWERPOINT GUIDE

Microsoft Office PowerPoint is a presentation software. We use this to create presentations and share them with students or other viewers. You can make presentations for your lessons or sermons, depending on what you want to present. In this guide, we will look at the main features of Microsoft Office PowerPoint. You will also learn about tabs and their tab groups. Each tab is divided into tab groups, with many command buttons for different tasks.

MS means Microsoft in short. I may use MS Word, MS PowerPoint, or MS Office in the guide, so you should know what that means. This guide is small, yet it simplifies the program, so that you can broaden your knowledge of its main parts and sections. When you need to do something, you do not get lost. You simply jump into that section and work like a guru. You will need Office 2007 or later in order to learn as you practice the lessons in this guide. Thank you for choosing my computer guides. You can now get the same guides all in one—**Basic Computer Knowledge** (this book).

MS PowerPoint Main Window

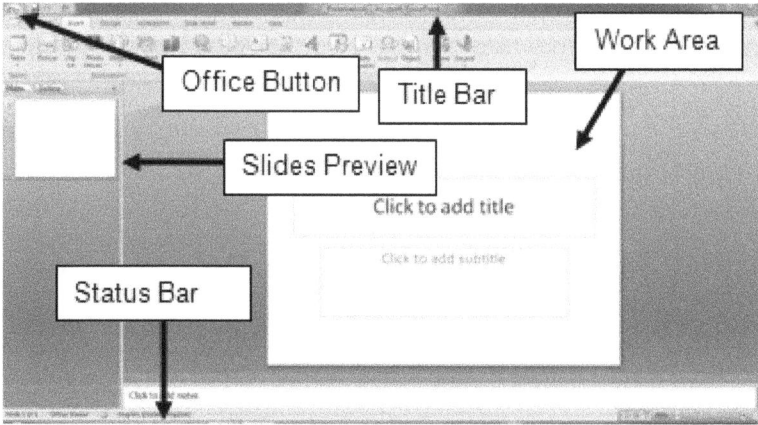

Figure 165: MS PowerPoint features

In this main window, you will see tabs such as Home, Insert, Design, Animations, Slide Show, Review and View tabs. You can see the slide pane on the left, work area in the centre, status bar in the far bottom and the title bar on the top part of the main window. Like any other MS Office program, the title bar of MS PowerPoint contains control buttons, Office Button and the Quick Access Toolbar.

Launching MS PowerPoint—there are many ways to launch any program in Windows OS. You can double-click the shortcut icon of MS PowerPoint on the desktop to run it, or left-click it if it is pinned to the Start Menu or Taskbar. Left-click the Start Button and check the Start Menu for MS PowerPoint icon. Not seen? Then click "**All Programs**," link => **Microsoft Office** => **Microsoft Office PowerPoint**. I hope you can see it now. If not, then MS Office or PowerPoint might not have been installed on your computer.

The main features of MS PowerPoint

Bars—Title bar, Status bar, Quick Access Toolbar, and Menu bar.

Tabs—Home, Insert, Design, Animations, Slide Show, Review, View, and other Hidden tabs.

Ribbon—this contains all command buttons needed for each task under each tab group.

Buttons—Office, Control, Help, and other command buttons.

CHAPTER 1: HOME TAB

~~**~~

Introduction—under this tab, you will learn about tab groups, such as **Clipboard, Slides, Font, Paragraph, Drawing**, and **Editing**. This is the most important tab to know more about in order for you to create your professional looking presentations. Here, you will do a lot of work with your presentation.

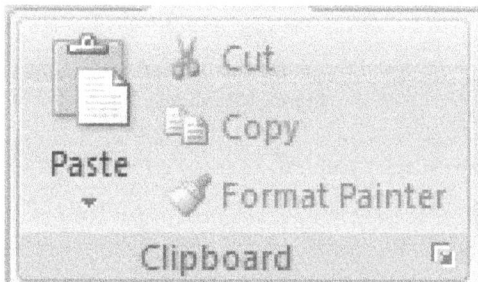

Figure 166: Clipboard

Clipboard Group—like other MS Office programs, here you can cut, copy or paste copied or cut text or an object to the document. The clipboard area holds cut/copied items until you delete them from there. You can choose many pasting options, using paste arrow. Use the **Format Painter**, to apply the same formatting to another text. This is helpful when you don't have to repeat the same formatting process each time.

To use a **Format Painter** tool, select the format you want to use on another text, and then click the **Format Painter** button in the ribbon as shown in the picture above, and then click on the text that you want to format, and that will be it. If the previous was **bold**, the text will be formatted the same.

Keyboard shortcuts—to copy, cut or past, you can use some keyboard shortcuts. The Ctrl+C will copy the selected text or picture. The Ctrl+X will cut the selected text or picture. Moreover,

251

the Ctrl+V will paste the selected text or picture into the document. These commands work in most text editing programs, even web browsers.

Figure 167: Slides

Slides Groups—under this tab group, you can create new slide, set the slide layout views, reset the slide to the default view, or delete the selected slide. To create new slide, click on the **New Slide** command button, as shown in the picture above. There are nine slide options to choose from. Click on the **New Slide** arrow to see those options. To delete any selected slide, select it and then click on the **Delete** button as shown above.

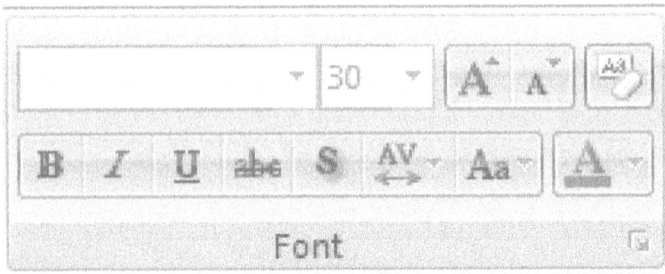
Figure 168: Fonts

Font Group—under this tab group, you can format your text as you can do in other MS Office programs, such as MS Word. Here, you can format the selected text bold, italic, underline, strikethrough, increase, or decrease font size, and change font shadow effects. You can also change the font colour and font face from here. You can also clear the current formatting, if you wish.

Please check out the class work PowerPoint guide with your instructor for more information on how to work with this tab group.

Keyboard shortcuts—to perform the same actions, you can use keyboard shortcuts, to make the work go faster. The Ctrl+B will make **bold** the selected text. The Ctrl+I will *italicize* the selected text, and the Ctrl+U will underline the selected text.

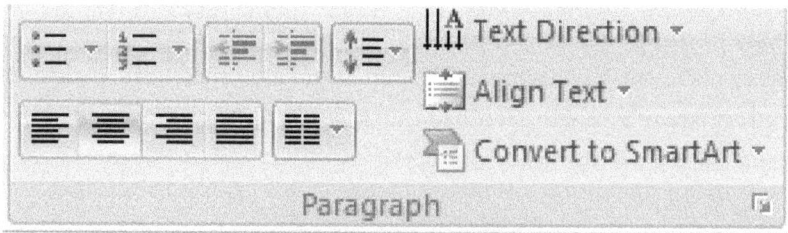

Figure 169: Paragraphs

Paragraph Group—under this tab group, you can use the text alignment features. You can align text or any selected item to the right, left, or centre. You can also justify it. You can indent the text and choose the line spacing. You can use the bulleted list and numbering features. You can change the text direction or convert the slide text to SmartArt. You can also align the text to the top, bottom, or centre. You can also set the column numbers from here.

Keyboard shortcuts—you can use keyboard shortcuts to perform the same operations. To centre the selected text, use the Ctrl+E, and to align the text left, use Ctrl+L, to align to the right, use the Ctrl+R, and to align the text as justified, use the Ctrl+J.

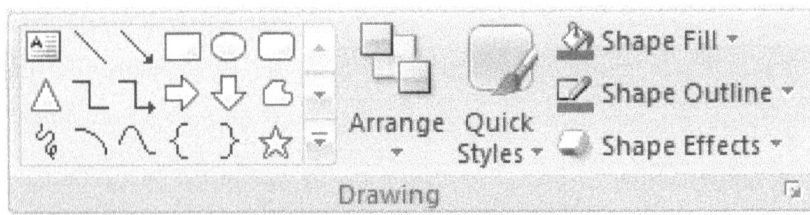

Figure 170: Drawing Group

Drawing Group—under this tab group, you can draw any shape in your slide. You can also arrange items, change the shape fill and shape outline colours. You can also change the drawing effects. To draw, click on the shape and then drag it somewhere inside the textbox area. You can also use quick styles to format your slides to make them look the way you like.

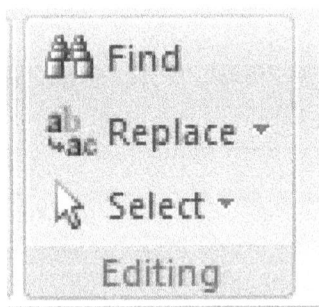

Figure 171: Editing group

Editing Group—under this tab group, you can perform certain actions such as **Find**, **Replace**, and **Select**. You can find text in your slides just as you can find text in your MS Word document. You can also replace text in your slides. You can also select all text, select an object, or open the selection pane from here.

Conclusion—we have come to the end of this first tab in MS PowerPoint. You have explored the tab groups under this tab such as Clipboard, Font, Paragraph, Drawing, and Editing. You have also learned that this is the most important tab of all, because you can do many things here with your professional presentations. Next, you will learn more about the **Insert Tab**.

CHAPTER 2: INSERT TAB

~~**~~

Introduction—under this insert tab, you can insert different items into your presentation. Here, you will learn how to insert **Tables, Illustrations, Links, Text,** and **Media Clips**. To learn how to do all these, kindly pay attention to what your instructor tells you. You will learn how to work with all these features practically, if you follow the instructions given during the class work. The instructions are now given in this guide, not only in the classroom. Just follow the steps below and you will be ready.

Figure 172: Tables

Tables Group—under this tab group, you can insert tables into your presentation. This is great, especially when you are presenting data and critical information, which needs good sorting. There are ten rows and eight columns by default, but you can increase the number by clicking on the **Insert Table** command button. You may like to draw your own table or insert an **Excel Spreadsheet**. For more help, ask your class instructor. You can also open PowerPoint now and play around with it. When you draw or insert a table, other tabs will show up, such as the design and format tabs. We will discuss those tabs later in the book. To draw a table, use the left mouse button to click and drag to draw lines where you want them to appear. You must do this practically.

Figure 173: Illustrations

Illustrations Group—under this tab group, you will learn how to insert illustrations into your slides. You will learn how to insert Pictures, Clip Arts, Photo Albums, Shapes, SmartArts and Charts as you can see in the picture above.

To insert a picture or any other illustration into your slide, just click on it. For your convenience, Excel program will open when you want to insert smart arts. It seems there are no keyboard shortcuts for these commands. This means you will have to click the command buttons on the ribbon as shown in the picture above. Some tools may be located in different places, depending on which version of MS Office you are using. The examples in this guide were taken from MS Office 2007.

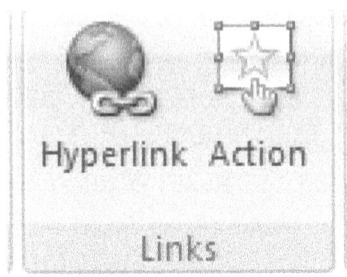

Figure 174: Links

Links Group—under this links tab group, you can insert hyperlinks and actions into your slide. Hyperlinks can link to a document or file in your computer, or to a web page on the Internet. You can even link to other parts of the same document. You can also bookmark some sections of your document to text or an item. You can also set actions, such as mouse click or mouse over. These actions can either run programs, link to other sections of the same document/presentation or other files, or play sounds when the user performs them. To link a webpage, select the text where you want it linked, and then click the hyperlink button as shown in the picture above. You will then type or paste the link into the address box that will appear, and then click the **OK** button. When the user clicks the linked text, the user will be taken to the webpage you have linked to the presentation.

Figure 175: Text

Text Group—under this text tab group, you can insert text boxes, header and footer, word art, slide numbers, symbols and objects into your presentation. You can also insert the date and time into your presentation. You can insert or draw a text box into your slides.

To learn how to all these things, listen to your instructor during the class work time. This means you can now practice the lessons alone. Open the PowerPoint program and create a simple presentation for your own practice. Try to insert a text box, header and footer, word art, date and time, slide number and so on and so forth.

Media Clips Group—under this media clips tab group, you can insert a movie or sound into your slide. A movie or sound will play when you view the slide. To insert a movie into your slide, select the slide where you want it to appear, and then click on the movie command button. Do the same to insert the sound into your slide. You can insert movie or sound from file or from the clip organizer. Again, do the real practice now. Play around with the media clips section until you discover other things not even discussed in this guide. Learning by doing is the best way to learn to discover new things. Good luck into your computer training.

Conclusion—under this tab, we have discussed briefly how to insert different items into your presentation. You have learned how to insert tables, illustrations, links, text and media clips into your slide, to make it look the way you want. You will learn all these actions practically during your practice time.

Next, we will look at the **Design Tab** and its tab groups.

CHAPTER 3: DESIGN TAB

~~**~~

Introduction—under this tab, you will learn how to design your slides as you want them to be. Under the design tab, you will choose from many predefined designs, which you can modify to make your work look professional and cool for your viewers. Under this tab, you will work with page setup, themes, and background tab groups.

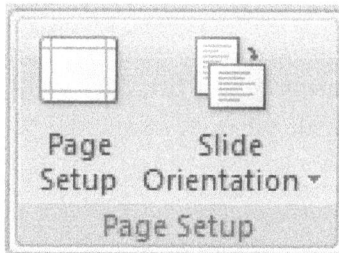

Figure 177: Page Setup Group

Page Setup Group—under this page setup tab group, you can change page setup and slide orientations. You can set slide orientation to **portrait** or **landscape**. You can also setup the width and height of slides in your presentation, right from here.

To learn how to do this practically, listen to the class instructor during the class times. On the other hand, you can play around with the tools right now. This is why you need the program to learn how to do these practically. This guide was written for students who were taking computer classes. I have then decided to make it available for other audience, so that they can make use of it. You are one of the audiences, so learn by practice, since you may not come to our physical classroom in South Sudan.

Figure 178: Themes

Themes Group—under themes tab group, you can change to any theme you like, as shown. You can change the colours, fonts, and effects. To apply a theme to your document, click on it and it will apply to your document. Each theme has its colours and fonts. To learn more about this tab group, please listen to your class teacher. You can now take some time to play with the themes section of your MS PowerPoint program. The section may likely look a bit different, if you are using MS Office 2010 or later. Play around with the tools until you create what you wanted.

Figure 179: Background

Background Group—under this background tab group, you can change the background styles and choose to hide or show the background graphics. You can format the background styles and choose fill or a picture as a background style.

To learn more on this practically, check the class presentations by your current class instructor. Alternatively, in your case, open the MS PowerPoint program from your computer and take some time to play with it. This will be great for you as you learn practically. I personally love learning by doing. Discovery comes when we test ourselves and make possible mistakes. So try now and learn by doing.

Conclusion—in this tab, you have learned about page setup, themes, and background tab groups. These tab groups contain commands that you need, to perform certain actions.

Next, we are going to discuss briefly about the **Animations Tab** with its tab groups. It seemed there were no keyboard shortcuts for these tasks. After creating your beautiful slides, you will need to animate them, to make them look professional on the screen. This is the work of the coming tabs and their tab groups. After you create your work, there will be time to show the work to your viewers, and you will need to make it look funny, and professional.

CHAPTER 4: ANIMATIONS TAB

~~**~~

Introduction—under this tab, you will learn how to work with animations to make your presentation look professional. Here, you will work with tab groups such as preview, animations, and transitions to the current slide. There are many animations to choose from. Animations make your work look funny, as well as professional to the viewers.

Figure 180: Preview

Preview Group—the preview tab group is used to preview your slides, as they will appear when presenting to your audience. Select a slide and then click on this button as shown above, to preview your work. However, you cannot preview until you entered text and selected one of the available animations.

Figure 181: Animations

Animations Group—under this animations tab group, you can choose from different styles of animations. The available styles are **fade**, **wipe** and **fly in**. You can also customize the animations to make your work look exactly what you want it to be. Click the arrow next to "**Fade**," and you will see more styles. You can also click on the "**Custom Animation**," button to customize your selected object or text the way you want.

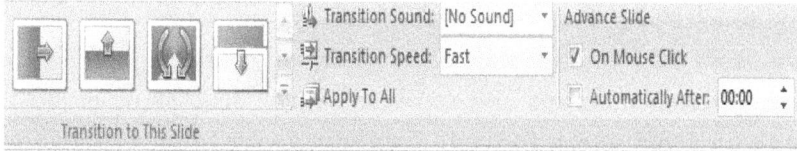

Figure 182: Transitions

Transition group—under this transitions tab group, you can choose from many available transitions for your text. You can also choose the transition sound, speed and apply the same setting to all slides, if you want to do so. You can choose whether the actions will happen automatically after a set time, or users can click the mouse first. That is it for the animations tab and its tab groups.

Next, we will move on to the slide show tab and its tab groups. These are the main features of the MS PowerPoint program. Exploring the tabs means learning almost everything about the program. This is in a very summarized and easy format.

CHAPTER 5: SLIDE SHOW TAB

~~**~~

Introduction—the Slide Show Tab in MS PowerPoint is one of the smaller tabs, because it has few tab groups. Under this tab, we will learn how to start slide show, setup slide shows, and how to use different monitors and resolutions. The slide show is mostly shown on full screen for your audience to view your presentations on a larger and wider screen than your own. Mostly, you will need a projector in order to show your presentations to your audience.

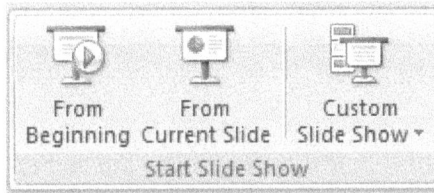

Figure 183: Start slide show

Start Slide Show Group—under this start slide show tab group, you can show your presentation to your audience, using a projector. You can start from the beginning, start from the current slide, or use the custom slide show option. To learn more, follow the class instructor's instructions during the class time. This means you can now learn by practicing the lessons. Click on the Slide Show Tab, and play around with the tools.

Keyboard shortcuts—you can start slide show, by using a keyboard shortcut. To start from the beginning, press **F5** on the keyboard. To start from the current slide, use **Shift+F5**. Keyboard shortcuts make your work quick and easy, but you have to be very careful not to press a wrong key combination. This may make the computer do something else, such as deleting or copying and pasting something.

Figure 184: Set Up

Setup Group—under this setup tab group, you can setup the slide show, hide the current slide and do other settings as shown in the picture above. You can record narration into the slides, use rehearse timings or set the rehearse timings.

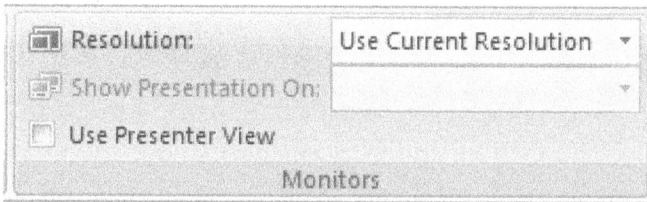

Figure 185: Monitors

Monitors Tab—under this monitors tab group, we can use the current resolution of the screen, or change it to any available resolution. The presenter view can only be used when you have more than one monitor connected to your computer. If you have more than one monitor connected, then you can show presentations on any of them as you switch from one to the other.

Conclusion—under this Slideshow Tab, you have learned how to start a slideshow, how to work with setup tab group, and how to switch to different monitors.

Next, we will look at the View Tab in MS PowerPoint.

CHAPTER 6: REVIEW TAB

~~**~~

Introduction—under this tab, we will learn how to use reviews before we finalize our presentations. Here, you can use the proofing, comments and protection functions of MS PowerPoint. Some of these features may not work on all computers. You can restrict access to your presentations, but this is not a free service, meaning you will have to sign up for it and pay after the trail period expires.

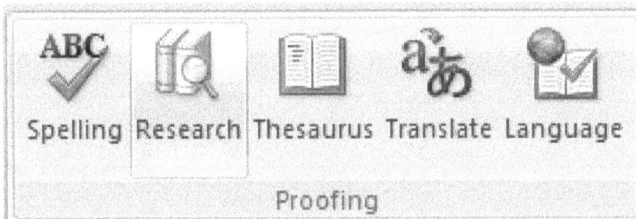

Figure 186: Proofing

Proofing Group—like in MS Word program, you can check and correct spelling errors under this proofing tab in MS PowerPoint. You can also research the meaning of words online, using the research functions. You can use a thesaurus to check other meanings of the selected word in your presentation. You can even translate your presentation from English to any available language. You can set the language to use for proofing and grammar checking. To learn more, kindly listen to your class instructor.

Keyboard shortcuts—to start a spelling and grammar checking, press **F7**. To open the research functions, press **Alt+Click**. To search for other similar words in the thesaurus, press **Shift+F7**. This is called keyboard shortcut or keyboard combinations. It makes your work easier than using command buttons in the ribbon as shown above in the picture.

Figure 187: Comments

Comments Group—under this comments tab group, you can insert comments in to your presentations, just like can you do in MS Word program. You can insert new comments by clicking the "**New Comments**," command button as shown above. You can edit comments, show markup or navigate to previous or next comments, if any. You can also delete comments.

This function is useful for those who want to review your work, and still want you to have a final say in the matter. You can then accept or reject their suggestions. You can do the same for someone else. They will have to reject or accept your suggestions.

Figure 188: Protection

Protection Group—under this protection tab group, you can protect your documents. However, as mentioned earlier, this may not work on your computer, because it is not a free service. You will need an internet connection, so that you sign up and subscribe to this service from Microsoft. If you love the service, then you can pay for it after the trial period expires. The good thing about this service is that it will protect your documents from others who may try to open them without your permission. However, getting the service requires some money.

267

CHAPTER 7: VIEW TAB

~~**~~

Introduction—under this tab, you will work with presentation views, show/hide, zoom, colour/greyscale, window, and macros tab groups. Most of these functions are similar to those in MS Word and other MS Office programs.

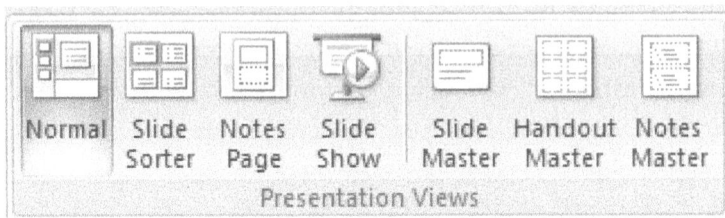

Figure 189: Presentation

Presentation Views Group—under this presentation views tab group, you can use normal view, slide sorter, notes page, slide show, slide master, handout master, and notes master. All of these are different functions that you can only learn practically in class. The normal view is selected by default as you can see in the picture above. You can even run a slide show from here.

To use a keyboard shortcut, press **F5** and it will begin to show your presentation in a full screen. You can exit this by pressing the **Esc** key on your keyboard, normally on the far left hand side.

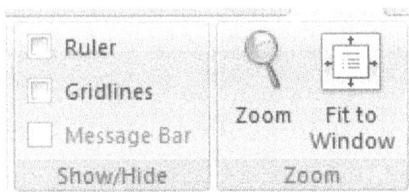

Figure 190: Show/Hide

Show/Hide—under this show/hide tab group, you can show or hide the ruler, or show/hide gridlines. You can also show the message bar. Under the zoom tab group you can zoom in and out or make the slide fit to window as you can see in the picture above. Use **Shitf+F9** to show/hide the gridlines in the presentation. This is the keyboard shortcut for that, which may work in all MS Office PowerPoint programs, I guess. Will it not work in yours? Try it and see how it will go.

Figure 191: Colour/Greyscale

Colour/Greyscale Group—this is a tab group, where you can choose colours for the whole slide or presentation. You can choose greyscale, pure black and white, or colour, as you can see in this picture above. To learn how to work with these features, listen to the class instructor during the class. Alternatively, play around with the tools right away. This is when you cannot make it to class for sure. You do not have to come to class as long as you have this book and the MS PowerPoint software installed on your PC.

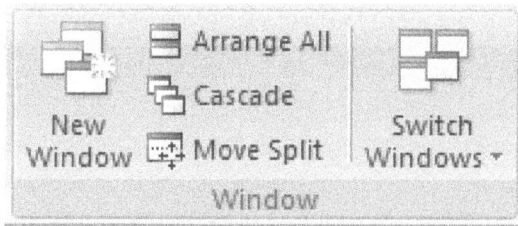

Figure 192: Window Group

Window Group—in the window tab group, you can view the presentation in a new window, arrange all windows, cascade windows, move or split a window, and even switch between multiple windows, if opened. You can only switch to a different presentation, if there is more than one of them opened. The split is done when you want to see different parts of slides and work at the same time as you present. There seems to be no keyboard shortcuts for those actions.

Figure 193: Macros

Macros Group—the macros tab group is not very important, but you may need to use it, sometimes. Macros are some functions or actions that you want your computer to take at a given time. I do not use macros, because they can allow you to run viruses on your computer, sometimes. You can create macros here, by clicking the macros command button, as you can see in the picture above. The keyboard shortcut for macros is **Alt+F8**. You can play with the tool, until you create what you want. Learning by doing is the best way to learn, so go ahead.

CHAPTER 8: OTHER HIDDEN TABS

~~**~~

Introduction—in any Office program, there are hidden tabs, which only appear when needed. The format and design tabs only appear when you need them. If you insert a picture or an object, such as shapes into your presentation, you will see additional tabs in the menu bar. In addition, if you have some add-ins installed, you will see the add-ins tab in the menu bar.

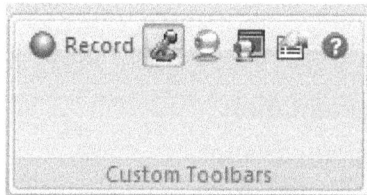

Figure 194: Custom tools

Add-ins Tab—this add-ins tab only appears when you need it. For this example, we have the add-in for **Camtasia Studio**, which can help you record videos of your computer screen for making computer tutorials. I use Camtasia Studio to create self-learning course materials in video formats. As you can see in the picture above, you can do many things with Camtasia Studio software, right on your MS PowerPoint.

Format Tab—when you insert a picture or an object to your slide, you will see the Format tab in the menu bar. Under the format tab, you can format picture styles and adjust the current picture by clicking on it. You can also arrange pictures with text in the slide. You can also set the size of the current picture. There are also many tab groups under this main tab with all their command buttons.

OTHER BOOKS BY JOHN

Autobiographies
- Journeying With God Part I-V
- Journeying With God Part I
- Journeying With God Part II
- Journeying With God Part III
- Modern Marriage and God
- Sudan Civil Wars
- The Scarification

How-tos
- Academic Orientation
- Affiliate Training Guide
- Author Training Guide
- Basic Computer Knowledge
- DP Publisher's Guide
- Internet Residual Income
- Microsoft PowerPoint Guide
- Microsoft Windows 7
- Microsoft Word 2007
- Payoneer Payments
- Publishing a Book on Amazon
- Self-Publishing Experience
- Ten Successful Ways
- The Editor's Guide 101
- The Marketing Guide 101
- The Publisher's Guide 101
- The Writer's Guide 101
- Using Microsoft Paint
- Windows 7 Control Panel
- Windows 7 For Beginners

- Windows 8 For Beginners
- Windows XP Control Panel

Life Coaching
- Humans
- Our National Heritage
- The Patriotic National
- The Principles of Conflict Management
- Thinking Bigger and Wiser

Literary Nonfiction
- 50 Funny Stories
- 50 Wise Words
- Beegu City
- Beyond Religion
- Life Cure

Poetry
- 2016 In Poems

Theology
- Evangelism and Discipleship
- Freed Forever!
- Life of Christ
- Lifted Up For His Glory
- Love Is Not Blind
- Synoptic Gospels
- The Book of Creation
- The Journey of Faith
- Welpieth Ke Yecu Kritho
- Your Self-Discovery Guide

For more information, visit this author's Facebook page at www.facebook.com/japshalom and then click on the **Shop Now** button.

God bless you!

Keep it #Shalom!

TABLE OF FIGURES

CPSIA information can be obtained
at www.ICGtesting.com
Printed in the USA
LVHW030320220222
711692LV00003B/113

9 781520 259314